The Love You Deserve

A Spiritual Guide to Genuine Love

Dr. Scott Peck
Shannon Peck

THE LOVE YOU DESERVE:
A SPIRITUAL GUIDE TO GENUINE LOVE
Copyright © 2002 by Scott & Shannon Peck

Lifepath Publishing
P.O. Box 830, Solana Beach, CA 92075

Cover by Robert Howard.

Printed 03 04 ♥ 10 9 8 7 6 5 4 3 2

Library of Congress Control Number: 2002090128

ISBN: 0-9659976-7-7

Publisher's Cataloging-in-Publication
(Provided by Quality Books, Inc)

Peck, Scott, 1945-
    The love you deserve : a spiritual guide to genuine
love / Scott Peck, Shannon Peck. – 2nd ed.
    p.cm.
    LCCN 2002090128
    ISBN 0-9659976-7-7

    1. Man-woman relationships. 2. Love. 3. Intimacy
(Psychology) 4. Caring. 5. Spirituality.   I. Title

HQ801.P43 2002   306.7
                                  QBI33-312

To

Kaia Phelps & **Connie Nguyen**

Our daughters in Love
May you each experience the love you deserve

and

**Our parents
Sis & Ed & Elaine & Sid**
for modeling genuine love

Gratitude

We give abundant thanks to Georgia Carter and Janet Lynn for their generous love & editing support of this revised second edition.

We also give gratitude to each member of our invaluable review team for the first edition: Patti Barnes, Sarah Battelle, Mary Jane Boyd, Virginia Byrd, Mark Harris, Chris & Kathy Faller, Bob & Sharon Griswold, Larry Jensen, Jill Lesly Jones, Janet Lynn, Justin & Katy McKinney, Patsy Neu, Connie Nguyen, Kaia Phelps, Dan Powell, Dan & Nancy Price, Jim Redington, Rebecca Smith, Nan Tellier, and Shaun Michel Winn. And very special gratitude to Collier Kaler who helped launch the first edition of this book as our publicist and treasured friend.

Contents

Love is Calling You

1. Your Spiritual Right to Genuine Love   9
   The Love You Deserve Quiz   15

10 Keys to Genuine Love

2. Loving Yourself   19
3. Friendship First   31
4. Kindness & Honesty Combined   45
5. Cherishing Each Other's Dreams   63
6. Listening To The Heart   73
7. Perpetual Intimacy   89
8. Genuine Equality   101
9. Empowering Manhood   119
10. Empowered Womanhood   135
11. Loving Out From Spirituality   149

Rising in Love

12. Finding the Love Mate of Your Dreams   157
13. Expanding a Relationship to Ultimate Love   173
14. Flowing with Love in Hard Times   181
15. Healing Hurt & Abuse   199

Chapter 1

Your
Spiritual Right
to Genuine Love

You deserve to experience all love.

This is not a dream or hope. This is your spiritual right. This is what Love wants for you.

If you are single, this book will clarify and lift your love standards and show you the path to the love mate of your dreams.

If you are already in a relationship – even a great one – this book will open your heart and mind to what is truly possible in love.

If you are struggling in a relationship, the light of Truth and Love in this book will bring your love life into great clarity – and move you towards the love you deserve.

If you think you are unworthy of being loved, or that it is too late and you will never truly be loved, let this book be a love letter to you personally.

Love is calling you
higher

The Universal Song
of Love

The vast majority of the songs of the world sing of our great desire to be loved.

Each of us yearns to be loved by someone who cherishes us, believes in us, names us as their special one, caresses our innermost soul, and empowers our entire being.

Can you envision yourself experiencing such love? Far too few of us can. Over 50% of marriages in the United States end in divorce. And how fulfilling are the remaining partnerships?

Our love lives beg for transformation! We need a breakthrough in our love consciousness – a vision powerful enough to bring us into a new dimension of the love we deserve.

Rising Higher
in Love

It took us, the authors, many years to open ourselves to the love we deserved. We're astounded that we could have lived so long in ignorance of our spiritual right to be genuinely loved.

Today, thank Love, we live in the utter heart and joy of genuine love with each other – as life partners, best friends, lovers, Soul mates, confidants, mentors, professional colleagues, and spiritual partners.

This entire book flows out from our relationship. Our desire is for every individual in the universe to experience the liberation, power, and joy of the love we experience every day.

We always knew that we deserved such love. In our ignorance, however, we both thought it would happen naturally when we married.

Well, it didn't. Each of us endured difficult, hurtful earlier marriages. We had assumed, naively, that we would be completely loved when we married. We weren't prepared for less. In our love ignorance, neither of us had a clue that genuine love was a *spiritual right.* We didn't know how to make decisions that would bring genuine love into our lives.

Through great struggles and deep prayers for many years, we each gained higher love ground. We both moved through separate divorces and the consequent struggle to see ourselves as undamaged and valuable.

This book is the outcome – the story – of the consciousness that led us to each other and the awareness of our spiritual right to be genuinely loved. Today, neither of us could imagine settling for less!

You have an immense opportunity that we didn't have. You can learn what it means to be loved genuinely by allowing this book to lift you to the consciousness of the love you deserve.

Each of us deserves such love. No one is excluded. If genuine love seems unimaginable to you, open yourself to this truth:

Genuine love comes forth
when consciousness
opens the door

The Power of
Holding a Vision

Each of us is being called to vastly higher ground in love – to see that it is our spiritual right to experience all the treasures of love.

Are you holding this vision for yourself?

We need to make a leap in love consciousness as big as society made in recognizing that women had a right to vote. Not very long ago, the vast majority of women and men did not *envision* that a woman deserved to vote. It had not entered *consciousness* as a possibility, much less as a spiritual right. It was not until 1920 – after great personal struggles, sacrifices, and hard work by visionary pioneers – that women were granted the right to vote in the United States.

"Granted" the right! Who granted this right? When were men granted the right to vote? Who granted men this right?

Do you see what truly took place? A great shift took place – in *consciousness*. Even though a few women and men understood and advocated this new idea, it didn't become a spiritual right until it was accepted in collective consciousness. Today, of course, this right is recognized and cherished almost universally.

Here is the big question: Weren't these rights *always* legitimate? Of course they were! But we first had to *envision* them as rights before they could become a reality. We had to admit the *possibility*!

This is exactly what needs to take place today in our love lives. Each of us is being lifted to a vastly higher consciousness of love. Our sense of love needs to expand exponentially. We need to admit the possibility of genuine love.

Our spiritual right to genuine love already exists – within each of us – waiting to be acknowledged and experienced. Looking back 50 years from now, let us not exclaim, "How could we have been so ignorant of our spiritual right to genuine love?"

You are not likely to experience love greater than your consciousness can conceive

Open the Door to Love

The dawning of a higher idea is often met with skepticism, but the issue is not whether genuine love is possible. The real issue is:

What is genuine love and how can I experience it?

As your thought opens to this spiritual right, the love you deserve becomes visible – and that's what this book is all about.

The only thing that can hold you back from genuine love is your own thinking. You can never be deprived of real love by another person – or any circumstance – because genuine love is already inherent within your being.

Experiencing genuine love is an agreement to live an awakened, spiritual life – to acknowledge and be who you really are as the precious creation of Love, worthy of both giving and receiving all of Love's treasures.

Open your mind to Love's infinite possibilities for you. Allow yourself the gift of admitting to your own thought:

I deserve to be
completely & genuinely loved!

10 Keys
to Genuine Love

What truly makes love work? What will bring your life into alignment with all of Love's possibilities?

In order to make the transition to a new love reality, we need a bold model – a model etched so clearly in our consciousness that we have no doubt where we are going or how to get there.

The 10 keys to genuine love in the following chapters will reveal to your inner heart what is possible and waiting for you in Love.

And, if you wish, the Love Quiz on the next page will help you take stock of and rate your present love state, whether you have a love mate or not.

Welcome to
The Love You Deserve

The Love You Deserve Self Quiz

Directions: Circle the number that best describes your relationship. If you are not in a relationship, circle the number that best represents what you expect from a relationship.

1.   I love myself well.

    1   2   3   4   5   6   7   8   9   10
Not at all   To some degree   Completely

2.   My love partner & I have a wonderful friendship as the core of our relationship.

    1   2   3   4   5   6   7   8   9   10
Not at all   To some degree   Completely

3.   We each treat each other with consistent kindness & honesty.

    1   2   3   4   5   6   7   8   9   10
Not at all   To some degree   Completely

4.   We listen deeply to each other's inner heart.

    1   2   3   4   5   6   7   8   9   10
Not at all   To some degree   Completely

5.   We cherish each other's dreams.

1   2   3   4   5   6   7   8   9   10
Not at all   To some degree   Completely

6.   We experience perpetual intimacy with
        each other.

1   2   3   4   5   6   7   8   9   10
Not at all   To some degree   Completely

7.   We treat each other with genuine equality in
        all aspects of our relationship.

1   2   3   4   5   6   7   8   9   10
Not at all   To some degree   Completely

8.   We each support & honor manhood that is
        empowering rather than dominating.

1   2   3   4   5   6   7   8   9   10
Not at all   To some degree   Completely

9.   We each support & honor womanhood that is
        empowered rather than subordinate.

1   2   3   4   5   6   7   8   9   10
Not at all   To some degree   Completely

10.   We   each   love   each   other   from   deep
        spirituality.

1   2   3   4   5   6   7   8   9   10
Not at all   To some degree   Completely

The Love You Deserve
Self Rating

Total Score: _____ divided by 10 = _____

1-2
Love Vacuum
Time for radical revision & new possibilities

3-4
Minimal love
Need to set much higher standards

5-6
Survivable love
Is this acceptable to you for the
rest of your life?

7-8
Decent love
Why not go for the gold?
What would make your love a 10?

9-10
Genuine love
Rejoice!

Chapter 2

Loving Yourself

Love Key #1

How well do you love yourself?

1	2	3	4	5	6	7	8	9	10
Not at all				Somewhat					Completely

Loving yourself has everything to do with experiencing the love you deserve. It frees your life energy so you can love another well and it also opens your heart so you can fully receive love.

Despite years of education and life experience, most of us fail miserably in loving ourselves well.

This great loss usually takes place within our private consciousness, hidden from the world – hidden even from the people who think they know us best. We are masters at hiding ourselves.

When we allow ourselves to live without loving ourselves, we sentence ourselves to an isolated prison cell of love deprivation. And, unfortunately, most of us are very mean to ourselves. We refuse to grant ourselves pardon – or even parole – from our own imprisonment.

In truth, your rating of how well you love yourself reflects the degree to which you *hate* yourself. That word may seem too powerful, but it wakens us to reality.

How can we possibly love another well while we hold ourselves in bondage to guilt, shame, and unkindness and let our inner critic work overtime? Under such conditions, how can we fully accept and enjoy a love mate's love of us? Or freely give the love within our being? We cannot.

It is time to let ourselves off the hook and let much needed self-love stream into our hearts and lives.

All the energy you are using in hate, neglect, or dislike of yourself is lost energy for experiencing a much more expansive love life. How can we even calculate the immensity of this loss of love!

***It is time for each of us
to rise to the consciousness that
knows – and accepts – that
loving ourselves is our spiritual right!***

The struggle to love ourselves is vital to our well-being and our love life. It is time to learn how to give ourselves the love we deserve – from ourselves.

In fact, if you loved yourself twice as much right now, how would you do it? That's such a powerful question that we have an exercise on the next page to help bring this forward in your life.

Your list might include lightening your load, giving yourself more comfort, releasing old habits holding you back, forgiving yourself, turning off the inner critic, calming yourself, taking a yoga class, practicing more holistic health care, praying for yourself, or simply taking quiet time to meditate.

Don't skip or underestimate the power of this exercise. It will bring great truth to the surface in your life.

Top 10 Ways to Love Myself Twice As Much

If I were truly loving myself, I would:

1. _____

2. _____

3. _____

4. _____

5. _____

6. _____

7. _____

8. _____

9. _____

10. _____

***What you have listed above is
the love you deserve***

—

from yourself

Loving Yourself Boldly

When we took this exercise, we were shocked that there were so many ways we were *not* loving ourselves well. We realized that we could be more bold, more visible in *being* who we really are, and far more kind to ourselves.

Here, for example, are some of the things we now do to love ourselves well as a result of this exercise. We:

- Meditate and pray for ourselves each day and often throughout the day.
- Identify ourselves and all others as Light beings, all on a divine path.
- Boldly love and live our highest, heart-directed life purpose without shyness, doubt, or guilt.
- Forgive ourselves and others quickly and replace guilt with floods of comfort and healing love.
- Give ourselves frequent love breaks to shake off stress and burden.
- Give great and continuous thanks for all our blessings, even in rough times.

Loving yourself is not selfish
Loving Yourself
is a bold affirmation
of the value
of your
life

Benefits of Loving Yourself Twice as Much

The benefits of loving yourself twice as much are extraordinary. You will be more joyous, liberated, empowered, ready to expand and unleash your vast potential, and – most significantly – ready to give and receive love at a much higher level. If this is not enough, think of these benefits:

- You will feel freer to express your honest feelings and desires.
- You will connect with greater intimacy with a love mate because you are no longer hiding your true self.
- You will experience greater laughter and happiness.
- You will find yourself being more loving and more loveable.
- You will feel united with Love and experience the joy of living out from – not up to – the love you deserve.

This is the life you deserve and it all begins with loving yourself well.

As you love yourself twice as much, you will radiate a multitude of love-increasing qualities – confidence, self-esteem, joy, playfulness, openness, boldness – that will attract higher love relationships or dramatically lift your present relationship.

Remember, you are not a victim of your circumstances. You are only one thought – one decision – away from loving yourself twice as much. Your consciousness alone is carving out your experience, so stand in your spiritual power and love yourself in your true magnificence. This is the love you deserve.

Ways of Loving Yourself Twice as Much

Here are some liberating and empowering ways to love yourself twice as much.

Affirm to Yourself "I deserve all love"

You deserve all love. Yes you do! Don't let any argument within yourself talk you out of this spiritual right.

Loving yourself is not just about you. It is about everyone you know. Doesn't your best friend deserve all of love? Of course. No one is outside Love's embrace and it is time to affirm this – for you and for everyone. This is a spiritual truth and we are simply waking to its reality.

Powerful spiritual affirmations of your right to love yourself create a mental, spiritual container large enough for this love to come forward in your life.

As you read these affirmations about you, let them speak to your inner heart. Accept them as direct messages from Love – what Love Itself is thinking about you and wants for you. Affirm to yourself:

I am Love's bold and loving Presence. This is my real identity. This is who I truly am.

I acknowledge that I deserve all love and I accept this with rejoicing as my spiritual right.

I acknowledge that loving myself is a bold affirmation and expression of Love itself.

I acknowledge that loving myself well is simply a shift in thought to a more spiritual view of "me" that takes place effortlessly, naturally, and permanently through Love's blessing. All negative views of "me" that I have been clenching – even for years – are released in Love's higher embrace and Light.

I affirm that Love – right now – is unfolding the love I deserve in Love's own surprising and magnificent way. I yield my old negative ways with humility and happiness to Love's much-higher unfolding.

I acknowledge that, as Love's very own Presence, my life blesses everyone I know and touch. I think and speak and act with the intelligence and courage of Love Itself and affirm that being united in Love only benefits – and cannot hurt – anyone in my life.

I acknowledge that all humanity deserves to be well loved – to see itself united in Love, loved and loving. I am envisioning all humanity in this genuine unity with Love and cherishing this as humanity's spiritual right!

As Love's precious being, I take my stand in loving myself, acknowledging that this is the highest way I can honor and live in oneness with Love.

I acknowledge again that I deserve all love and I accept this with joy as my spiritual right.

Ask Again – Even Higher
What Would I Do If I Loved Myself
Twice as Much?

Go to a private spot that feels like a sanctuary and allow yourself, in utter stillness, to *feel* the safety, power, and joy of truly loving yourself. Then ask yourself again:

What would I really do
if I truly loved myself twice as much?

Be bold. Let go of restrictions. Love yourself as Love loving Itself. Make a great list of the things you would do if you loved yourself twice as much. Don't hold back. Love is calling you!

Many individuals live so far below this level of loving themselves that they do not even *think* about loving themselves twice as much – so they stay locked in old, non-loving habits of thought.

Those of you reading this book who are living in the midst of love abuse or love misery will be tempted to exclude yourself from the possibility of loving yourself twice as much. We know. We have been in that spot. Yet loving yourself is the way out of misery – even misery that seems beyond our control.

So expand your list. Don't allow anyone to talk you out of this. Feel the power of Love embracing you and calling you to your new Love home. Quietly take time to cherish what you have written. You have taken a gigantic step. You are envisioning higher love and that is the first key that opens your life to the love you deserve.

Loving yourself
is the path to freedom

Post Your Love List
So It Remains Visible to Your Heart

Loving yourself well is a lifestyle, not a momentary event. You deserve to love yourself continuously – so prepare to become an expert at this.

Post your top 10 list of ways to love yourself where you will see it all the time. Think of this list as:

- Your *most important* assignment to advance your life in love.
- What you can do today to live at your highest level of identity.
- A Love gift from Love Itself

Don't let your list slide into oblivion. Let that list jump out at you from your mirror, brief case, computer, purse, wallet, or car and say:

Yes!
It's time to love myself
with the love I deserve &
I'm going to do it right now
& continuously!

Change and upgrade your loving yourself list often. If your goals seem too big to implement, put one small section into action – right now! You are establishing a *pattern* of loving yourself well. Transformation begins with a single step.

Notice how many items on your list do not depend on anyone but you. This is good news!

Share Your Love List
With Your Love Mate or Friend

Sharing your love list with a close friend or love mate has powerful results. Sharing of your list, even if it feels awkward:

- Shows your love mate or friend your commitment to loving yourself.
- Affirms to *you* that your ways to love yourself more are important.
- Creates more intimacy with your love mate or friend, allowing you to connect at the core of your being.
- Enables your love mate and friend to know what is in your consciousness – and how to support you more effectively.
- Acts as a supportive influence to encourage your love mate or friend to make his or her own list.

If you are in a difficult relationship with a love mate, it may not be easy or possible to share your list. So be it! Don't let that stop you from loving yourself forward. Instead, share your list with a close friend.

Practice
Loving Yourself

Practice loving yourself. Doesn't that sound like a good – and powerful – idea?

Imagine the outcome of sustained practice of loving yourself! Practice brings us closer and closer to the love we deserve.

It doesn't matter if you mess up in practicing to love yourself. We all mess up in learning anything new. Love is calling you – and that call will never cease. Love Itself is lifting you to the mountain top of love possibilities. Your real practice is to accept Love's opportunities every single minute.

During our lifetimes, we all change – a lot. Often, however, when we take new life steps, it seems like a gigantic and awkward adjustment. Look back at who you were ten years ago. Have you changed? Amazing!

What is more important than to be advancing in love? You have enlisted in the healing process of carving out a more beautiful and fulfilling love life.

No matter what your old patterns have been, start loving yourself right now. Honor your inner worth. Let your heart's desires breathe. Cherish your gifts. Treat yourself with tenderness, gentleness, and forgiveness. Open your heart and listen. Love is calling you to the mountain top.

Wouldn't you encourage your son, daughter, best friend, or love mate to take this step? Of course!

Align Yourself
With Love

As you take the healing love steps presented in this book, you will begin awakening to your true relationship with Love.

You are *one* with Love. That is the amazing and most astounding reality about you. What this means to your love life is nothing less than transforming, for the love you deserve is not outside you – perpetually just out of reach.

The love you deserve is within your inner being because you are, in fact, Love's being. You were created by Love and therefore you can never be outside Love's embrace.

We all walk
in the midst of sacred love souls
You are one yourself

As we come into our spiritual light and shine it brighter, our Love light attracts others who are spiritually-minded and, together, we fuse our lights and experience oneness through Love.

And it all begins with loving and encouraging your own inner light to shine. This extraordinary truth is the sacred path to the love you deserve because it calls, not for circumstances to change, but simply for your consciousness to open to who you already are. So, let your Light shine!

Let yourself feel your unity with Love. Sense your Oneness with Love. You are finally coming home – and home is Love itself. How could you not love yourself if you and Love are One? Do you recognize that this is Love Itself talking to you, loving you?

We rejoice with you as you open your life to so much more love by loving yourself well. We stand with you, holding the space for you. Love is standing with you – and within you.

Loving Yourself
is Love's wonderful gift
to your life

Chapter 3

Friendship First

Love Key #2

Friendship at the core is one of the inner secrets of genuine love.

Think of the best friendship you have ever had. In true friendship:

- We are richly valued.
- We feel safe to be ourselves without guilt, shame, or manipulation.
- We share our feelings, dreams, and needs with honesty, openness, and kindness with each other.
- We laugh easily and freely.
- We are listened to thoroughly.
- We are not judged or condemned.
- We care about each other's well-being as much as our own.

The benefits and joy of true friendship are extraordinary. No games. No need to impress each other. Freedom to be our inner selves. Supported in exploring our dreams. Mental comfort. Honoring. Easy, open self-expression.

Can you envision your most intimate love-relationship including such a wonderful friendship? This is the real picture of the love you deserve – friendship at the core.

Genuine, successful love is rooted and grounded in deep friendship. In fact, when you say to your inner self, *"I deserve a bond of friendship with my love mate and I will accept no less,"* your love life will take a dramatic step forward.

If you sacrifice friendship with a love mate, you are not likely to experience all the love you deserve. Let's look squarely at one of the top derailers of friendship – and love.

The Deceit of Physical Attraction

We are hypnotized by physicality.

Second by second, we are subjected to a mental onslaught of sexually-oriented ads, dialogue, and pictures – in magazines, on TV, in movies and videos, in the songs we listen to, and in the conversations we hear around us.

We are so mesmerized that we are duped into a craving for the beautiful pinup woman or hunk of man. We dream, yearn...dream, yearn...and dream, yearn...until this love desire becomes a fixation. And we think this is normal!

It's normal, all right, like divorce, tears, abuse, and destroyed relationships have become normal.

Each of us deserves so much more than a shallow relationship based primarily on physicality and sex.

Of course we deserve to be loved – richly and passionately – in all ways. But physical attraction cannot sustain genuine love. A love relationship based *primarily* on physical attraction has devastating consequences:

- Who you are in your inner soul will remain unknown, smothered, and forever unexpressed – because you are likely to be afraid to risk losing your relationship by revealing your true self.

- The relationship is likely to end, at some point, in one of you being physically attracted to someone else. One of you will end up hurt.

- There is likely to be tension, anger, frustration, disillusionment, and fighting because a physical relationship cannot bear the stress of all that naturally rises to the surface in a genuinely intimate relationship.

"But I want passionate love!" you cry. "I want fireworks and sizzle!" And you deserve it!

Even better, you can have it!

But sizzle won't provide lasting happiness without solid friendship first at the base.

This is the great deceit of relationships that hope to build from sex-up rather than friendship-up. Genuine friendship is not something that can simply be tacked on after a physical relationship is in full swing.

Physical attraction without friendship
cannot sustain the heart and soul
of genuine love

Friendship First
A Win-Win Love Strategy

Friendship first is the guaranteed win-win strategy for your love life.

When friendship evolves into passionate love, it has the rich substance that fires pleasure deep within our soul – and this pleasure is enduring.

When friendship does not evolve into a love relationship, you still end up with a new friend. Either way, you will feel satisfied *and* empowered.

Be honest with yourself. Without friendship, what chance does a love relationship have of being truly fulfilling and enduring?

None!

You deserve the great pleasure of passionate love that blossoms *within* a bond of genuine friendship.

But what happens if a potential love mate wants to zing into passion mode and come back to friendship later? Or expresses no interest whatsoever in a bond of friendship?

Don't compromise! This is the exact moment – the turning point in your love life – that will determine the quality of love you will experience in that relationship.

If you let down your standard of developing a strong, genuine, loving friendship in exchange for a passionate evening, it will be extremely difficult – and maybe impossible – to experience genuine friendship later. Commit to friendship first and let your wonderful friendship develop into time-tested and mutually-committed deep affection before moving into love.

It is so tempting to compromise – because we all want to be loved so badly, and right now! By taking this stand, you may fear that you will give up all possibility of ever being loved, or that you will be forever lonely, but just the opposite will happen. You will open your life to higher, richer, and more fulfilling love.

Don't sell yourself short! You are worthy of all love. Affirm to yourself:

"I am deeply worthy
of being well loved & I deserve
a bond of friendship with my love mate
and will accept no less!"

When you take a stand for a bond of friendship in your love life, it is an invitation at the highest level for the love mate you truly deserve to step forward.

Finding a love mate
is not a question of time,
place, looks, talent, or opportunity

—

Meeting a love mate
is a question of the love standards
in your own consciousness

Scott's Love Story

Here are Scott's words about his own love life when he finally woke up to genuine love.

After I was divorced, I felt unworthy and sad that I would probably never experience the genuine love I thought would simply be a natural part of my life. Even though it was an enormous relief to be finished with an unhappy marriage, I knew I had a lot of love to give. Why shouldn't I be loved as richly as I knew I could give love?

I soon came to an inner conclusion: I would rather remain single forever than ever again be unhappily married. I knew right then that I had crossed an important inward marker. I had decided that if I were ever to remarry (which, to be honest, I doubted), my own needs and dreams deserved to be richly valued and loved. I thought to myself:

I deserve to be well loved!

This idea empowered my entire inner life and sense of self-esteem. It felt good to love myself enough to claim such love.

Over the next months, this idea kept strengthening within me until, finally, in the privacy of my own consciousness, it exploded in Light. I thought to myself, *"What I'm feeling is even bigger than deserving to be **well** loved."*

I deserve to be perfectly loved!

This was astonishing to me. Never in my life had I envisioned this idea – this spiritual *right* – to be genuinely, thoroughly, perfectly loved!

I felt the power of this idea so keenly that I knew right then it was inevitable that I would experience genuine love – even though there was no one special in my love life at that time. I was as sure of my right to genuine love as I was that the sun would rise the next day.

**When you take a stand for genuine love,
your love experience will rise
to your new expectations**

I knew that time and circumstances had nothing to do with it. My consciousness had risen to an entirely new dimension. I was absolutely sure of success in experiencing my right to the genuine love I deserved.

Several weeks later, while training a large group, one of the participants in the back raised her hand and asked a question. I didn't know her, but I immediately felt, "This is the one."

Later, however, when I asked who she was, I was told that she was married – so I didn't contact her.

Weeks later, I learned that she was actually divorced. I called her and with simple honesty, said: "I met you recently at a workshop. I don't know if you remember me (she did), but I felt led to call you. I think we need to know each other." She was rushing out to an appointment when I called and asked if I would call back.

Well, I didn't.

Even though I had come to the conclusion that I deserved to be genuinely loved, was I right to intuit so strongly that this was the person?

As some of you may understand, living through a marriage where I was not esteemed or cherished, my feeling of self-worth was still recovering. I was also just leaving for a three-week photo trip in Turkmenistan and Uzbekistan in Central Asia with a fellow photographer and friend.

During those next three weeks – completely isolated from the rest of the world or any communications – I continued to feel the clear presence of my new-found right to be genuinely loved. It was a quiet awareness in my consciousness. I now understood that this right was inherent within me. It was a powerful sense of love. I felt I was *already* experiencing genuine love. I'll never forget it. This is what it taught me:

The consciousness of genuine love precedes the event

When I returned to work, there was a message waiting – would I please call her.

We met that weekend – the beginning of a bond of friendship and unity that expanded to the immense love I now enjoy with Shannon, my extraordinary wife and love mate.

Shannon's Love Story

Here, in Shannon's own words, is her simultaneous love story.

When my ex-husband left me after eighteen years of marriage, my self-esteem was at an all-time low. I was devastated, even though it had never been a happy marriage. The pain was almost unbearable. Even though my own profession is spiritual healing, my emotional needs seemed overwhelming.

I began working to heal myself, working each afternoon in my office, while my phone was quiet. I'll never forget the first afternoon I did this.

When, for the millionth time, I felt prompted to feel devastated, I went into a mode of bold and powerful affirmations based on my deeply held understanding that I am spiritual.

My affirmations specifically challenged and replaced unspiritual thoughts I was thinking about myself. Whatever I needed at the most fundamental emotional level, I turned into a powerful affirmation. All my affirmations came forth from my highest understanding of spiritual Truth.

For example, I boldly declared to my consciousness – just as you can – such truths as:

- Love is seeking me out and claiming me as its own, saying, "You are mine! You belong to me!"

- Because Love is ever-present, I am always in the full, living presence of Love – and I know it and feel this Love here and now with me.

- The entire area of my consciousness that appears to be so dark is actually filled with great Light. I am in this Light. I live in the splendor of this glorious Light!

- Because I am spiritual, I am singled out by infinite Love and labeled worthy of praise and adoration. I feel and see Love rejoicing over me, celebrating me.

- Divine Love is announcing my great goodness to all humanity, and all humanity is responding to me with love. I see Love manifesting to me in infinite ways right now. I feel totally secure and safe in this Love.

- Because I am spiritual, Love has a wonderful plan for me that names me in the plan as absolutely essential. Love makes sure I am aware of this.

- I feel Love loving, embracing, providing, upholding, encouraging, and directing me every step, every moment.

- I am guided, comforted, and protected by Love. I feel secure with all life's changes because Love is the governing, intelligent power of my life.

- Because I am spiritual, I am being husbanded by God. God is my husband and He is naming me as his glorious wife, worthy of His love. Together, we share in this radiant light of Love. I am never alone.

Sometimes, as I stated these and many other affirmations, I would giggle and laugh out loud. These affirmations were so far from my experience that it seemed ridiculous to state them as true.

However, I was accustomed to going to the divine core and making bold statements of Truth – and later seeing their supremacy and power rule the situation. I trusted my spiritual reasoning implicitly.

Within a short while, the expression of Love began to fill my life. A couple of wonderful men appeared in my life, one of whom I thought was "Mr. Right." Another was Scott.

There was something unusual, however, about my friendship with Scott – it was a true bond of unity. I could feel how deeply he cherished whatever was most important to me.

Because of his honoring, my fears and doubts about being committed began to wash away. New hope rose within me. I slowly came to trust the genuineness and quality of Scott's love as the true manifestation of my spiritual affirmations.

I told "Mr. Right" my heart's true knowing. I needed to let my relationship with Scott unfold in the magnificence of what I knew was answered prayer.

I know that Scott and I found each other through divine Love, the source of all love. I found that I could completely trust divine Love's law of attraction and cohesion to govern my entire life – including my love life.

Love is seeking you out
& claiming you as its own, saying
"You are mine!
You belong to me!"

Establishing Friendship
with a Potential Love mate

"What can we do to ensure that our relationship will be grounded on true friendship?"

That's the question we asked ourselves when we became instant friends, began dating, and it became obvious that the relationship could easily evolve into much, much more.

Even as we wondered how this relationship would unfold, a deep truth was speaking to us in our private consciousness:

If this friendship is meant to be love,
nothing can stop it

—

If this friendship is meant to be
only friendship,
cherish the friendship

This is a powerful affirmation. It unites us with Love itself. We relaxed in the consciousness of this truth and relished the wonderful friendship we were experiencing. We knew that we could no longer settle for less in any love partnership.

What happened next was phenomenal. Our friendship grew to awesome power for each of us. We experienced the depth of a bond of unity:

- We spoke to each other with complete honesty and openness, no matter how embarrassed we felt. We didn't hide our feelings about anything. This was a joint decision early on.
- There were no games. No playing with each other's feelings. No manipulation.

- We listened deeply to each other's feelings, needs, and desires – by the hours.
- There was extraordinary and reliable kindness.
- We laughed freely and continuously, enjoying the freedom of our friendship.
- We honored each other's accomplishments and life insights.
- We didn't judge each other. We both felt deeply valued for who we really were.
- Through an unconditional respect for each other's individuality, we discussed our inner dreams.

Can you envision how good this felt?

As weeks passed in the enjoyment of this friendship, it was obvious that a love relationship was developing and deepening.

What would happen to our friendship during this transition?

Holding On to Friendship
When Love Takes Over

Can friendship and romance develop together?

We knew a turning point had arrived as the love we felt for each other grew stronger. Would our friendship now change? Would it be compromised?

As friends, we felt total liberation in sharing our feelings. We had nothing to lose. We were living within a bond of friendship. That is what we both needed and wanted. Now that love was surfacing, it became more challenging to be honest. We found ourselves privately thinking:

"If I reveal my true feelings, I might appear stupid or weak and less loveable – and I may lose this love opportunity."

This thinking, of course, if acted out, would have quickly destroyed the bond of our open friendship.

Deep within, we recognized that we would rather lose each other as love partners than have a love relationship, however beautiful, devoid of genuine honesty.

We felt both empowered and scared feeling this way, but there was no other choice. So we spoke the truth – thinking, more than once, that the truth could cause our budding love to wither.

For example, during this period, Scott felt frustrated in his occupation. He feared, however, that if he shared this openly, our potential love relationship might be lost. He was afraid this would make him less attractive.

But our friendship was too important to sacrifice. So he shared his feelings, revealing his real inner self. And he was shocked by Shannon's reaction. She loved him more! And she deeply appreciated his openness.

Shannon also had a concern early in our courtship when Scott asked her, *"What do you truly want in your life?"* Did she dare say it? She pushed open the doors of honesty and said, "I want to get married again one day." She felt she had put everything on the line by being so open. But Scott didn't retreat!

We both answered the question, *"Am I willing to give up friendship for love?"* with a resounded *"No!"* We wanted *both* and knew that we deserved both.

The immense closeness of our friendship empowered each of us. As we each encouraged more of such liberating honesty, we found greater and greater unity – and more love!

We can't begin to tell you the exhilaration of experiencing this love within the context of a bond of genuine friendship. It is not just that our love grew stronger. Our friendship flourished just as powerfully. We felt the liberation of friendship *and* love.

This is the friendship in Love you deserve as well – and it begins deep within your consciousness.

> ***Friendship first***
> ***is the guaranteed win-win strategy***
> ***for your love life***

Chapter 4

Kindness & Honesty Combined

Love Key #3

Kindness & honesty combined are awesome in their power to liberate love. They need to be expressed *simultaneously* for two good reasons:

- Without kindness, honesty stings the heart and causes us to retreat from love.
- Without honesty, kindness feels empty and untrustworthy and leads away from intimacy.

Expressed together, kindness & honesty bring enormous benefits to love:

- Both partners feel safe because kindness is always present.
- Both partners are in full touch with each other's hearts because honesty is also present.
- Intimacy is vastly increased because both partners are able to reveal inner desires, feelings, hopes, fears, and vulnerable feelings in a supportive & honest environment.

This combination of kindness & honesty is one of the potent secrets of genuine love.

Is It Really Possible to Combine Kindness & Honesty In a Love Relationship?

It certainly is!

In fact, we need to see kindness & honesty combined from the highest spiritual perspective.

If you take kindness to its highest meaning, you arrive at Love. And if you take honesty to its highest meaning, you arrive at Truth. Hence kindness & honesty combined are really a fusion of divine Love & divine Truth in action.

Love & Truth are inseparable and are never expressed without each other. This, of course, reveals the spiritual power of kindness & honesty combined and why they lift a relationship to infinite happiness.

So why are kindness & honesty combined as one force so uncommon in our love lives?

- Because so many love mates expect far less and have never been taught this powerful love skill.

- Because so many individuals have never seen or experienced the modeling of consistent kindness & honesty combined.

- Because so many love partners have discovered that they can get away with unkindness and an absence of honesty without serious consequences.

The tide in love relationships, however, is turning. Love partners are waking up. The lack of kindness & honesty is being recognized as an outdated mode of love thinking. And until you understand that unkindness and a lack of honesty are not love, you are likely to tolerate, accept, and experience them.

We must rise in our consciousness of love to understand that we truly deserve to experience the peace and support of sustained, combined kindness & honesty. Anything less than this is a sham on love. Good looks, wealth, dazzling opportunities, and sizzling moments cannot overcome the internal havoc and disaster of unkindness and lack of honesty.

> *"Come on now, Scott & Shannon, don't you two ever act with unkindness to each other?"*

No, we don't! Even during life's biggest storms, we maintain our kindness to each other. We draw the line that protects love. We are so grateful to no longer be in past marriages which included unkindness that we treasure the kindness we experience with each other as much as the oxygen we breathe. We count on it. We are committed to it.

Kindness is the oxygen of love

Our kindness stems from our great love for each other and our view of kindness as the natural expression of divine Love. To be unkind violates our deepest understanding of who we are as expressions of Love.

We falter, of course, and there are times when we hurt each other's feelings, but not often – and never deliberately. On stressful days, we stretch to be kind and respectful – even as we work through emotions.

We usually sense when one of us does or says something that hurts the other, and we act quickly to correct our words or actions rather than let hurt take on a life of its own. We seek to discover why the other is hurt, and we make sure our larger love for each other is always acknowledged.

We are also willing to change our behavior if that is what it takes for the other to feel loved, but we are also true to ourselves. This is the fine balance where kindness & honesty combined have great healing power.

We work quickly to rise above negative talk or thinking that would let us wallow in hurt, frustration, or anger. We know that holding on to such feelings shatters joy, intimacy, and the sweetness of our partnership. We have learned not to be self-destructive. Here's a typical example.

While we were engaged, Shannon had been thinking about getting her first computer. She was leaning towards a Mac because of its reputation for being easy to use.

Scott tried to steer her towards a PC because that's where he was experienced. We had several discussions where we respectfully (Scott thought) disagreed.

Well, one evening, Shannon phoned and announced that she had decided to buy the Mac – and she asked Scott not to try to talk her out of it. She said she felt like a little flower being crushed by a ten-ton steamroller on this issue.

Scott was caught off-guard by her strong feelings.

It is at such a love-juncture that genuine love needs to excel. What seems like a simple issue can escalate into a power struggle, a control issue, or a feeling of alienation.

Scott immediately told her how much he honored her right to make whatever decision she wanted – and that he understood the appeal of the Mac. He listened as she explained that she had just come out of an 18-year marriage of domination on such decision-making. This computer choice was one of her first decisions to make on her own.

Scott felt terrible. He had vastly underestimated the impact of Shannon's previous marriage on her well-being. Instantly, he switched sides. Scott knew that her right to make her own decisions was the central issue and cherished her right to be independent.

Scott told her that his motivation in suggesting a PC computer was not to control the decision, but to help us connect our lives more intimately by sharing compatible computers and equipment that he understood. His motivation was to be as completely unified as possible and he shared this.

Sensing his depth of honoring for her, Shannon also switched sides, realizing the choice was not about control and domination. Scott's kindness & honesty combined spoke volumes to her and cut away a history of being controlled.

The issue was never a computer. The real issue – to Shannon – was her right to make her own decisions. The real issue – to Scott – was his desire to be as unified as possible with Shannon.

Our kindness & honesty combined brought these real issues to the surface to be known – and healed. Anger or frustration would have buried the real issues and our love would have paid the price. Today we happily share compatible computer systems – and Shannon made the final decision.

There are many ways to bring the empowering combination of kindness & honesty into your love life. One way is to ask a very simple question:

***What are you thinking
Sweetie?***

This powerful, delicate question instantly shows your desire to connect with your love mate.

It asks for honesty, but if asked with kindness, it opens a gentle path for sharing and an instant uniting of hearts.

Even with kindness, however, this question is so honest and open that it can catch a love mate off-guard. One might privately feel, *"If my love mate knew what I was really thinking right now, I'd be in trouble! I'm not emotionally prepared to share my thoughts."*

Yet here is the exact moment where kindness & honesty combined can come to the table with great healing power.

For example, suppose that you have been working overtime and you just sat down in the living room with your love mate, not thinking too seriously about anything, but you sense that your love mate is thinking deeply about something, so you ask: "What are you thinking honey?"

And suppose your love mate responds:

> *"I'm feeling that you have been distant and wrapped up in your own life. It's as if you don't care and I don't matter. I am not feeling very loved."*

And you're thinking:

> *"Oh great. I just sat down to unwind. If I had known this was coming, I would have stayed in the other room."*

This is one of those significant turning points in a love relationship where your response will make a huge difference to the quality of your love life – for a long time.

Let's look at three possible answers to your love mate's words:

Answer 1:

"What the heck do you expect me to do, stop doing my job well? I'm under a lot of stress. Get off my back!"

Answer 2:

"Honey, I'm buried to my eyeballs in this project. I have no choice. Can't this wait?"

Answer 3:

"Sweetie, I love you. I'm sorry you feel this way. I have a lot of things on my mind that are distracting me, but let's take a moment to share our thoughts together. I want you to know how much I love you."

You can easily chart the impact of these answers on a love relationship.

Answer 1: This answer is honest, but with harshness, frustration, and anger. Even if given in the first flush of feelings, this answer slams the door on real love and raises all the defense shields. How many times can you or your love mate survive this answer and still consider yourselves as "loving" each other? If you presently lean towards responding to your love mate this way, begin to change your habit now – and offer quick apologies.

Answer 2: This answer is honest, but without much empathy. It shows a focus on yourself and excludes your love mate's needs. Without kindness, even when it's inconvenient, how often will your love mate want to ask the question, "What are you thinking, honey?" Goodbye intimacy.

Answer 3: This answer is honest *and* kind. Rather than an emotional knee-jerk response, it shows compassion for your love mate and recognition that discussion is needed to solidify your love. It may be emotionally difficult to immediately come up with this answer from your heart, but it is worth whatever internal struggle it takes to get to this depth of love.

Every single time you
act with kindness & honesty
you increase your skill with this powerful
love force and uplift your love life

It's Not Easy
to Come Out of Our Shells

Love mates often exist together like two ships passing in the night – unseen and unknown.

It takes great kindness to navigate the waters of deep intimacy and bring us out of our shells. It also takes great honesty, and this very honesty reveals the emeralds waiting to be discovered in the depths of each other's love. When these gems are left unmined, love withers. Scott knows! Here are his own words:

In my previous marriage, I did a lousy job of speaking out openly with my feelings. I felt extremely vulnerable. When I did muster the strength to speak from my inner heart, I often felt scorned, ridiculed, or emotionally ignored. Behind the listening, I felt a hidden wave of anger and disgust to my responses.

Not too surprisingly, I retreated into the privacy of my own mental shell. As any good Star Trek fan will understand, when you have to divert most of your life energy to your shields (defense mechanisms), you don't have full power for your main systems. I was operating at minimal life power.

Today, I am married to Shannon – and what a difference! Because of her consistent kindness and encouraging love, I now speak openly from the heart. We even have this book as evidence!

What Shannon did was extremely liberating to me. More than anything else, she created an environment of great kindness. Whatever I share from the heart is cherished, listened to, and discussed with great honoring. You will hear more about this in the next chapter, *Cherishing Each Other's Dreams*.

How did Shannon do this? With combined kindness & honesty. She expressed such easy acceptance, joy, honesty, spiritual honoring, and laughter that my heart melted into openness. I found myself more and more able to reveal my inner self because of her modeling of kindness & honesty combined.

Kindness
Like a River of Love

Here's what our kindness means in Shannon's words:

As Scott and I dated and became instant friends, I experienced his massive, dependable kindness. I have never known anyone so kind and gentle. In fact, my daughter Kaia described Scott as the power of softness and gentleness, like the waters that carved out the Grand Canyon. The first week we were married, it felt like perpetual heaven – and it still does!

One evening, early in our marriage, I got up to go to the bathroom. As I returned, Scott passed me in the hall and whispered "I love you honey." Even in the middle of the night, his kind words and sweet tone of voice assured me that all was well and that I was loved.

This daily kindness is what we call "speaking heaven" to each other. Kindness is indispensable to happiness in love and flows like a river with an infinite, continuous outpour of refreshing love.

Kindness & Honesty
flowing as one force is the language of
Love heaven

The Consequences of Unkindness & Lack of Honesty

The consequences of unkindness and lack of honesty are devastating to love:

- We feel disconnected from our love mate.
- We feel uncertain.
- We live only with the shell of the person we call our "love mate" without knowing what that shell really contains.
- We lead increasingly separate lives emotionally and intellectually.
- We clam up our thoughts and feelings for fear of ridicule, abuse, or disinterest.
- We raise our shields in self-defense of our fragile dreams and needs.
- We feel a well of resentment, hurt, and anger escalate within our heart and spill over to our love life.

- We seek out friends to share our pent-up feelings and needs rather than open our hearts to our love mate.
- We may be attracted to other relationships that offer kindness & honesty.
- In short, we don't feel loved!

These terrible consequences are not easily undone. If a love mate treats us with unkindness in one instance, how can we ever feel emotionally safe? And if a love mate is not open – or lies on even one issue – how can we believe there will be truth on other issues?

Love is so fragile.

Our dreams, needs, feelings, and ideas are like tiny roots that need tender nourishment – and nothing nurtures love like the combined force of kindness & honesty.

When Kindness & Honesty Are Abused

With so many marriages ending in divorce, kindness & honesty combined may seem an impossibility in our love lives. But shouldn't this jolt us awake?

We need a massive shift in consciousness and behavior if genuine love is to survive. That's what this book is about.

Those love mates who blame, condemn, criticize, dominate, control, have temper fits, swear at their love mates, demean their love mates, or physically threaten their love mates will likely recoil at the words in this chapter – in either shame or dismissal.

Those love mates experiencing such blame, condemnation, criticism, temper fits, demeaning language, actions, or threats will read the message of this chapter and likely turn to their mental pillows with hidden tears.

Our compassion for any individual lacking an environment of combined kindness & honesty runs deep. It motivates this book.

- It is your spiritual right to be treated with kindness and honesty. This is real love.
- Accept no less than consistent kindness & honesty with your love mate. Let this book guide you both to higher ground.
- If you are the one not expressing kindness & honesty, face down this enemy or you are likely to lose your self-respect and your love mate as well.

It is not easy to draw the line in love. But a *pattern* of unkindness does extensive damage to our love lives and cannot be ignored. This is not the love you deserve. Love is calling you higher.

Kindness & honesty
combined
heals wounds, binds hearts
& uplifts love

What's Stored In Your Barrel?

A powerful mentor once told a story:

"Imagine a large barrel, full of oil. What would come out if someone knocked a hole in the side of this barrel?"

Obviously, oil.

"What would come out if the barrel were full of water?"

Obvious again, water.

> ***Envision***
> ***Your own consciousness***
> ***as a barrel, full of whatever***
> ***feelings and thoughts***
> ***are currently***
> ***in your thinking***

Suppose, for example, that your consciousness is half full of love and half full of anger. And then suppose that your love mate comes along and asks you a probing question. What will come out?

Inevitably, love *and* anger.

Do you see the power of what is in your barrel – your thinking – right now? The combination of love and anger existed *prior* to the event. Here then is a healing insight of infinite value in relationships:

> ***Your response to any event***
> ***exists***
> ***prior to the event***

Now envision a different outcome. Suppose that early this morning in your quiet meditation, you worked to release all anger, fear, or doubt clinging for life in your consciousness. You did this because you understood their destructive nature if left to mix in your barrel. You did your best to have nothing but kindness & honesty in your consciousness. You recognized that this would create an environment for maximum love with everyone you encountered today.

And then the events of the day unfold. What will come out as you respond to events?

Of course, kindness & honesty combined – because they are *already* established in your consciousness!

This is potent, healing information for love mates. It means that if we take the time to fill our thinking with kindness & honesty, this is what will come out, even when we are caught off guard.

As we fill our barrel with love, our consciousness becomes an enormous defense system – already established – against reacting negatively to events.

Realistically, is this possible? It sure is!

True or false? Some people just get angry. That's the way they are. They can't change.

FALSE. We are each in charge of our thoughts and actions. Old habits of reacting with anger or unkindness may be hard to break, but our determination to express an empowering flow of love will lead us, with practice, to express greater and more consistent kindness & honesty with our love mate.

This commitment on the part of both love partners enormously strengthens the bond of love.

Here's a simple and revealing spiritual exercise. Draw a large circle on a sheet of paper and think of this as a barrel representing your consciousness.

Then write down in the circle, with great honesty, what is in your consciousness – the good and the negative.

As you become aware of the good, give yourself credit. As the negative appears, begin to release it as something that does not truly belong to you. Let it go so that more of your true Love identity can appear. Let your higher awareness remove what you know doesn't belong in thinking. Fill your barrel with the qualities and substance of overflowing love.

Some negative thoughts, of course, have a persistent way of sneaking back into the barrel of consciousness, but keep pushing them out.

Such prayer, meditation, or Love-cleansing enables us to bring to our day – and to our love mate – the full, healing force of kindness & honesty combined.

Kindness & Honesty
treasured and stored in consciousness
create an inevitable flow of
maximum love

Kindness & Honesty Combined in Action

Here are love-promoting *actions* that you can take right now to bring combined kindness & honesty into your love life:

1. **Make a clear decision** in your own mind to be kind and honest to your love mate and to become an expert with this love skill.

2. **Ask yourself**: How can I express more kindness & honesty combined to my love mate?

3. **Practice being kind & honest – right now.** Initiate a conversation with your love mate with this motive in mind.

4. **Ask your love mate**: *"What are you thinking, honey?"* Listen and respond with all the combined kindness & honesty you can generate.

5. **Respond with kindness & honesty**. Whenever your love mate asks: *"What are you thinking, honey?"* use this as an opportunity to practice and refine your love skill of combined kindness & honesty.

6. **Be alert** to when you fall short of kindness & honesty and decide how you can improve next time.

7. **Maintain a flow of kindness & honesty combined** in your love life. See if you can last one hour! One whole day! Better yet, commit to a life-time of combined kindness & honesty and watch your love life leap to new heights.

8. **Wait! Think!** When a testy moment surfaces with your love mate, think: *"Right at this second is an opportunity for me to practice honesty & kindness."* Do it! Give yourself the satisfaction and self-empowerment of rising above stress, a bad mood, hurt, defensiveness, anger, bad news, fear, doubt, or tension. This is the real test – the moment when kindness & honesty are most healing.

9. **Communicate your feelings.** If you feel your love mate is not being kind & honest with you, share your feelings with your love mate. Practice kindness & honesty yourself. For example, you might say:

   "Sweetie, I'd like to discuss something that's important to me. I want us to feel closer to each other. Can we discuss this so both of us can feel more loved?"

10. **Give this book to your love mate.** If you want your love mate to have a greater understanding of the value of

kindness & honesty, share this book
with the thought:
*"Honey, this is a book that has been very
helpful to me. I'd appreciate your reading
it so you will know what is in my heart. I
think this book will help us strengthen
our love for each other."*

11. **Surround yourself with friends** who
treat you with kindness & honesty.
Those who we associate with have great
impact on our lives, so surround yourself
with high-quality love models. We also
need to receive big doses ourselves of
kindness & honesty, so don't let yourself
get cut off from a world waiting to
support and love you.

12. **Affirm to yourself** that it is your
spiritual right to give and receive
kindness & honesty combined in your
relationship. Affirm: *"I am worthy of
being treated with kindness & honesty –
and this is how others deserve to be
treated by me."*

Kindness & Honesty
combined
bring the healing Light of Love
to our love lives

Chapter 5

Cherishing
Each Other's Dreams

Love Key #4

Our dreams power the universe.

Within each of us are vast, creative dreams. We dream of what we would like to be, do, and accomplish. For most of us, however, these dreams lay buried within the secrets of our inner soul. Our dreams are sometimes so fragile that we are too embarrassed to reveal them – sometimes even to ourselves.

It feels frightening to reveal them to those around us. What would they think? Crazy, egotistical, stupid – from another planet? Who are we to have such dreams? Yet these dreams persist in our private consciousness.

Nothing liberates the inner core of who we are as much as a love mate who cherishes our dreams and loves us so deeply that our richest, deepest identity is brought to the surface, recognized, and gloriously valued. Genuine love liberates our dreams.

Each of us
is like a gem
at the bottom of the ocean
hidden by layers of
timidity and accepted limitations

Shannon's Dreams Cherished

Here are Shannon's own words:

For many years I had a growing desire welling up deep within me – of tidal wave proportions – to reach out to the whole universe and share the greatest truths I have learned through my spiritual healing practice. I felt that the gems of healing I had learned would give others maximum comfort, inspiration, freedom, and healing. My heart was bursting with enthusiasm to share. I deeply wanted to end suffering through healing.

Though I had lectured and published articles, I still felt that I had not reached the larger audience of spiritual seekers that I could most benefit.

Scott repeatedly told me how much he loved that I am a spiritual healer – and his continual support felt terrific. Scott listened to my heart deeply and we both trusted that Love's plan would emerge – and it did.

I had never even considered teaming with Scott to do this work, yet we found a natural progression in speaking together about the principles of healing Love. Through our books, articles, workshops, and my widening healing practice, people came to us who I had longed to help for so long.

This fulfillment occurred because Scott cherished my dreams so fully and because we both opened our hearts in maximum receptive prayer.

As a woman, I had never experienced having my dreams equally cherished as a man's. Not only did this bring forth all the creativity within me yearning to be released, but it created a relationship of immense, flowing, open, sweet, and empowering love. And it took nothing from Scott. In fact, it brought him great joy to cherish my dreams. This is the love you deserve. And this is the love you will experience as you establish this love standard as your own.

Scott's Dreams Cherished

Here are Scott's own words:

I will never forget Shannon's liberation of my own private dreams.

Sitting in front of the fireplace at her home, in the first winter of our love, I felt her joy and the power of her caring. She asked me what I most desired in life.

In an instant, I silently reviewed my whole life – my hopes, dreams, failures, accomplishments, discouragements, present circumstances, choices, and possibilities – and came to a mental standstill. I felt I no longer knew what I truly desired. I was too discouraged to answer. I had no happy answer within me to give her.

Right then, Shannon declared:

> *"Let's affirm, right now that you can know your highest purpose in life and that nothing can prevent that idea from coming forth in full completeness and visibility."*

Wow! I was not accustomed to such a powerful and loving affirmation.

Later that evening, still feeling Shannon's cherishing of my invisible dreams, something clicked so clearly in my private consciousness that I jumped for a pad of paper. I felt so appreciated, valued, and loved by Shannon that my fears, shame, confusion, inadequacies, challenges, and doubts vanished in my consciousness. Her listening and non-judgmental love called forth my true identity and caused a paradigm shift in my sense of who I was. I felt the real me awakening. My dreams poured forth and were a revelation – even to me!

> *"I feel compelled to write a book that will open people to the love they deserve. I envision seven new rights advancing in consciousness as we enter the 21st century and I want to share them with the universe."*

To my own amazement, these seven rights spilled out on my yellow pad with what seemed to be 100% clarity to my inner senses.

I felt like a completely new person. Something deep within my consciousness had come to the surface. I felt that my life path had surfaced with great clarity.

Today, you are holding in your hands the book that is the first fruit of Shannon's cherishing of my dreams. *The Love You Deserve* is the outcome of our bond of genuine love which simply could not be contained and needed to be shared, as co-authors, with you.

Yes!
Your Love Mate
Does Have Dreams!

Don't think for a second that your love mate does not have dreams. Each of us is full of great richness.

Any time you think this is not true of someone, take 15 minutes with that person, forget yourself completely, and immerse yourself in listening actively to that person's heart and dreams. You will experience a fountain of creativity pour forth from the very soul of that person and you will have met a beautiful new friend. This is a powerful exercise.

Your love mate may claim to have no dreams, but don't believe it. When Scott was a counselor at an adult education center for disadvantaged adults in New York, a young woman applied for admission. When he asked her, with great interest and compassion, what she wanted to accomplish in her life, she looked at him, sensed his honest caring for her, even though they had just met, and began crying. She cried for some time.

Scott gently asked her why she was crying and she said: *"You are the first person in my life that has asked me that question."*

She then spilled out her dreams, feeling embarrassed to even have them, not sure she was worthy to dream. Scott cherished her dreams with her and encouraged her. She had taken a step much higher than simply enrolling in a class.

An environment of
genuine love, kindness, gentleness,
caring, & patience allows dreams to surface

This is the environment that genuine love seeks to create for *each* love mate.

In Shannon's many years of healing practice, she has found, over and over, the powerful and life-enhancing healing that comes forth when she cherishes the dreams of those who call her. Most have no realization that they even have a dream, yet, through much cherishing, their dreams always surface, bigger than life, there all along.

As a spiritual healer, Shannon has been a long-time dream cherisher because so much healing unfolds through honoring of another's inner desires. Cherishing another's dreams unlocks their beautiful divinity and Soul path and says to their heart, "Yes, It's worth it. Keep going. I'm with you."

Genuine love calls for great caring, gentleness, and patience as we cherish the dreams that we *know* are there. Real love is internally committed to the revealing of our love mate's dreams – and nothing throws us off course, even a love mate that insists, *"I have no dreams!"*

If you or your love mate think you have no dreams, this is your golden moment to relax in your love mate's cherishing and let your dreams surface in your consciousness.

- Perhaps you were never allowed to dream.
- Perhaps you were called stupid.
- Perhaps you have been considered subordinate.
- Perhaps you consider yourself to be inadequate.
- Perhaps, perhaps, perhaps.

Genuine love dismantles all these roadblocks and dissolves the mental and emotional chains that bind us from feeling free to dream, aspire, be, and listen to our innermost desires.

So start asking probing questions – with great love – and you'll discover a gift of Soul in your midst. It doesn't matter if your love mate's dreams come forth awkwardly or vaguely.

- Practice the listening skills in the chapter *Listening to the Heart* – and be quiet!
- Provide an environment of tenderness, caring, freedom, and patience and your love mate's dreams will focus into elegant beauty.

- Always, always assume that there is a dream and keep the space open for that dream to emerge.

Do you see the bigger event taking place as you cherish your love mate's dreams? The big event is even more than your love mate's dreams coming to the surface. The big event is that your relationship with your love mate is being transformed to a vastly higher level of love.

***When a love mate cherishes our dreams,
we feel the divine presence
of Love Itself***

Relish & Include
Your Love Mate's Dreams
as a Vital Part of *Your* Happiness

As you listen to your love mate's dreams, take an even higher step than listening.

Relish – as part of *your* happiness – these dreams. Incorporate your love mate's dreams into your own unfolding life.

What if your love mate's dreams do not interest you? This is not uncommon for many relationships. Unfortunately, these love mates often grow and mature in separate, unknown worlds to each other.

In genuine love, our love mate's dreams and ambitions are so important to us that we get involved in thinking about them too – and this involvement wakens us to their value.

Here's an example: Shannon is so satisfied in her full-time occupation as a spiritual healer that when Scott listens to her heart and cherishes her dreams, her love of healing spills out like an ocean overflowing with joy. We both find ourselves valuing even more deeply what she is doing – and Scott advances in his healing awareness.

This valuing doesn't mean that two lovers must have the same occupation or dreams. But it does mean that they feel connected to each other's hearts – to each other's passion and life purpose. This creates an enormous bond of love.

One day, Scott wanted to be sure he was in touch with Shannon's inner heart so he asked her if she had any other dreams.

"No," she said, but then rather tentatively added, *"except maybe to paint well."*

Scott doesn't paint, but he treasured Shannon's desire with enthusiasm and encouragement. Today – to our mutual delight – our home is graced with many beautiful paintings by Shannon.

Here's another example: Scott loves photography – and Shannon has strongly encouraged this passion. Her cherishing and nurturing of Scott's dreams led him to attend several weekend photo workshops that he never would have attended without his dreams receiving such tender support. These workshops vastly transformed his photographic skills.

Says Scott, *"I learned more in three days than I had learned in the past 20 years. I learned so much, not just because the workshops were effective, but because I felt the power of Shannon's enormous support and love for all I wanted to be."*

The most unexpected outcome took place from our joint cherishing. Scott began using his photos to make cards and then began adding messages – expressing spiritually what the images meant to him.

Well, that led to the spilling out of our immense inspiration as co-authors of this book.

This is the cherishing of inner dreams that you and your love mate each deserve.

Your Dreams
Are Just as Important

Don't ever believe that it is your role to provide an environment for your love mate's dreams to surface, but that it is not equally your right to experience your dreams coming forth.

In most love relationships, one member is often subordinate. This is a love travesty. In genuine love, such inequality is unthinkable!

Let you heart accept this affirmation, *"My dreams are just as important as my love mate's dreams or anyone's dreams."*

**It is your
spiritual right
for your inner dreams
to be cherished & honored**

Chapter 6

Listening
To The Heart

Love Key #5

Has anyone ever truly listened to you – listened to you with such focused attention and reverence for what is in your inner heart that you felt completely understood?

Most of us, unfortunately, are rarely listened to at this depth – by anyone, including our love mates.

The power of true listening is awesome:

- It opens mental and emotional doors.
- It tells us we are loved.
- It enables us to know ourselves.
- It opens our lives to revelation.
- It creates enormous intimacy.
- It bonds us together.
- It satisfies our heart and soul.
- We feel loved.

Yet so few people listen. So few know *how* to listen. What a loss!

***There is no greater gift
than to listen to your love mate's heart***

How many people in your entire life have listened to your heart? Go ahead, count them. How many people can you name who truly know what is unfolding in your private consciousness *right now*?

Does your love mate?

Do you even know what it feels like to be truly listened to?

Let's find out right now.

What's Going On
In Your Heart Right Now?

Allow us the privilege of listening to you – right now.

Even though we are not physically present with you, we are real persons speaking to you from the heart. And we are good listeners. So imagine that we are with you right now. Slow down your reading for a moment and silently ask yourself:

> *What is honestly going on in my heart right now? What am I quietly thinking within my deepest, private consciousness about my life at this moment?*

♦

As you prepare to share with us whatever you wish to share, we are looking at you with great caring. We are offering you complete and quiet space to think and share without interruption. We are listening with love and interest. There is no hurry to answer. There is no judgment.

♦

We genuinely want to know what is going on in your heart. In our verbal silence, we hope that our eyes are showing you how much we care. We honor you. We want you to feel the freedom to unpack whatever concerns, desires, or doubts you wish to share. Go ahead. Speak to us silently or out loud.

◆

As you gather your thoughts, we are tempted to say something – to make you feel more comfortable, to get you started, to agree with you, or to add our own feelings or thoughts to what you have said – but, no, we resist.

Instead, we stay in the mode of active but very quiet listening – in attentive, loving silence – allowing you the freedom to continue unfolding what is in your heart, even though it may be slow in coming out.

◆

As you slowly open to us – and yourself surprised to find yourself with so much space to speak without interruption, judgment, or direction, we continue to relish this moment of listening to your heart. Your long pauses test our listening skills because silence is awkward...

but oh so beautiful!

In silence,
the heart opens

We have learned the skill of silence and we happily present this gift to you. Please continue unfolding what's in your heart.

◆

As you speak, we are naturally tempted to let our internal thinking shift from you to *us* – to *our* life, *our* reactions to what you are saying, *our* conclusions, *our* expectations of what you will say next, and *our* judgments.

But we remind ourselves, internally, that true listening only takes place when we focus only on what *you* are saying, not on our reaction, judgment, or conclusions. We mentally return to you.

◆

As we make the effort to successfully stay tuned to your heart, we find ourselves feeling so much closer to you. We are beginning to truly understand you. Your heart is speaking to our heart. It is an extraordinary experience – for *us* – to listen so openly and non-judgmentally.

◆

As we continue listening to you without the distortion or noise of our lives, we begin to discover the depth of what is truly taking place in your heart. We are in awe! You, too, are in awe – almost disbelieving this enormous space of freedom to let your heart come forward. Do you have more to share?

◆

Our continued silence opens the door for you to share more. Your heart now appears with increasing clarity, but then you come to a stopping point.

- Is this the end?

- Are you getting annoyed at too much listening with no feedback?
- Should we break this long and silent listening?

We think these questions privately, but communicate to you with our eyes and heart that we want you to feel the freedom to do whatever your heart delights. We do not want to interrupt your inner flow.

This may be a pause of self-discovery. You may have more to say. We do not want to break the silence that allows you the freedom to continue without diversion. If there is more within you that needs to come forth, we want you to have the experience of all that is within you being cherished.

◆

The silence between us is sacred. We see you searching your heart at even greater depth. Our highest love at this precious and profound moment is continued quietness.

You continue speaking.

And we continue listening with unconditional acceptance. We want to understand, not judge.

You are almost unaware of us now, continuing to explore and speak at even greater depth. Inwardly, you are surprised that anyone has listened to you so thoroughly – allowed you so much space to unfold.

You reach another end point. We sense that you have had the opportunity to say all you wish to share for now. We see your satisfaction in getting so much of your heart out in the open. We see the dawning of your realization: *"So this is what it feels like when someone truly listens to your heart!"*

Thank you for opening to us. Isn't this wonderful? Your heart has opened wide and shared it's fondest treasures.

Real listening
says to our love mate
"I cherish deeply what is in
your heart"

We truly wish we could sit with each reader of this book who has never experienced such listening. But now you know what you deserve. Each of us needs the satisfaction – the healing – that pours forth during such listening.

- When was the last time anyone listened to you with such tenderness, quietness, thoroughness, and genuine interest?
- When was the last time your love mate listened to your heart in such a way that you felt satisfied in sharing all that was within your heart?
- When was the last time *you* listened to your love mate – or anyone - with this quality of honoring, liberating listening?

To feel understood
in your inner heart is to experience
genuine love

The Secrets of Listening

The secrets of listening are simple – but little practiced. When others listen to our heart with love:

- They are quiet.
- They don't interrupt.
- They don't lead us or control where the conversation goes.
- They don't interject.
- They don't judge.
- They are experts at empathy.

They listen ever so quietly – with such a great desire to understand us that we can feel this caring.

When we pause to ponder our own thoughts, they don't break the silence. They listen even to our silence, telling us without words that what we are saying is valuable. They quietly support us in getting it all out.

We don't feel judged – because we are not being judged. When we think we have finished speaking, we pause, but there is no interruption.

We feel free to speak – unfold – even in silence or awkward attempts until it is clear that our heart has spoken openly and completely. We feel loved by the genuine focus that seeks to know and cherish what is in our heart.

Most of us seldom experience anyone listening to us this way. Next time you are with friends, or with your love mate, mentally think about what is taking place. Ask yourself:

- Does anyone care about what's in my heart?
- Is anyone listening to my heart?
- Am I listening to another's heart?

In a relationship based on genuine love, both love mates yearn to understand each other's hearts, not just during courtship, but forever. This is a continual commitment.

How fast does it take for your love mate to be out-of-touch with your feelings, ideas, dreams, and plans? Minutes, not days!

It is astounding how fast our internal thoughts of life – our feelings, ideas, desires, plans – change. If you listened to your love mate yesterday, that's little guarantee that you are still in touch with his or her heart today.

Underneath all this discussion of listening, there is one skill that outshines them all for staying in tune with your love mate's heart – the skill of empathy.

Become an Expert at Empathy

To become an expert listener, you have no choice but to become an expert at empathy.

Empathy means that you listen so thoroughly and non-judgmentally that you really do understand your love mate's words and feelings – and your *love mate* feels your genuine understanding.

There are many "appearances" of listening, but empathy is the real thing. For example:

- We can listen – and have no idea of what someone just said.
- We can listen – while we inwardly respond in anger, disgust, jealousy, or judgment.
- We can listen – while we are inwardly engrossed in preparing our response.

None of these qualify as real listening. To put it another way, how would you feel if someone listened to you in any of these ways? Not well honored! And certainly not well understood.

There are many kinds of listening and it would be unproductive and frustrating to always listen intently to your love mate without speaking out yourself. Most conversations are give and take sharing.

There are times, however, when our hearts yearn to sing and be heard – or when we need healing love. These are the times where empathy unlocks your love mate's heart and conveys pure, liberating love.

Empathy
with genuine caring
is the key that unlocks the heart

Here are some steps that will enable you to become an expert empathizer and connect with your love mate at a much deeper level.

Decide
to Listen

This is a giant decision.

It means that you decisively enter your love mate's world and leave your own world of thoughts, needs, activities, and planning for the time being.

There is no half-way position. You either tune in to your love mate or you miss the boat. Most people miss the boat. Why?

Because most of us are so engrossed in our own thoughts, needs, interests, priorities, and feelings that we rarely make this love leap into another's heart. Also, we are not practiced in settling ourselves into a pattern of stillness and quiet listening.

It takes great unselfishness and genuine caring to make this transition, but when you do, you will have taken a love leap that transforms your relationships.

If you think this is easy, try listening to someone right now with full empathy. Check how quickly you are sidetracked by your own internal thoughts.

Tune in Non-Verbally

Listen to your love mate with your mind and body – not with your mouth.

Tune in non-verbally to your love mate and show your interest and respect and love through direct, encouraging eye contact and body language.

Few people communicate with direct eye contact. You might be surprised how difficult it is to look your love mate directly in the eyes.

Direct eye contact
shows a desire to be intimate

Try this experiment. The next time someone is supposedly listening to you, check out their eyes and see how often they wander and glaze. You will begin to appreciate the power of body language.

It may seem subtle to you, but even a small shift of body and eye language tells your love mate that you have wandered off mentally into your own world, no longer truly hearing.

Faking doesn't work. Even if you think you are successful at faking good listening, your love mate will have already sensed this lack of genuine connection and will have stopped communicating from the heart. You may still be hearing words, but it won't be from your love mate's inner heart.

To put it another way, you can't fake real love.

- Do you really want to listen?
- Do you really care?
- Are you honestly prepared to tune in?

These are the questions your heart, eyes, and body will answer.

Listen With Unconditional Caring

What happens when you visit a good counselor or therapist? You are listened to with empathy and unconditional caring.

- The counselor listens with full body attention.
- The counselor listens without judgment.
- The counselor truly wants to understand you.
- The counselor cares for your well-being.
- You feel this love and you slowly open your heart because of the environment of unconditional caring and non judgment.

For many people, the only person who has ever truly listened to them is a counselor. Isn't this a shame? Why should you and your love mate be deprived of such powerful, liberating communication with each other?

As you let the ideas in this chapter sink into your consciousness, you will not only become an expert listener, you will also become an empowerer. You will discover the immense joy of empowering another person through genuine listening.

***To listen to your love mate
without judgment
is one of the
highest forms of love
you can give***

Name the people in your life right now who *listen to you* with unconditional caring and no judgment.

- ◆ _____
- ◆ _____
- ◆ _____
- ◆ _____
- ◆ _____

Now name the people in your life who *you listen to* with unconditional caring and no judgment.

- ◆ _____
- ◆ _____
- ◆ _____
- ◆ _____
- ◆ _____

You may have very short lists!

You can enlarge your list immediately by simply opening your heart to the desire to listen genuinely.

Here's what you can do right now:

Put this book down and go listen with un-conditional caring and without judgment to your love mate or a friend. Let your very being communicate the following message:

"I want to treasure what's in your heart. I am actively listening to you right now –

*caring for you with no other motive than for
you to feel understood and have the
opportunity to share with me what is in
your heart.*

*I want you to feel the full freedom of
communicating with me in an environment
of total non-judgment.*

*I want you to feel honored and accepted as
you are."*

Use The
Power of Silence

How do listeners most rapidly fall off the bridge of good listening? By opening their mouths – even when their intentions are admirable.

**As soon as
you open your mouth
real listening
stops**

Here's what happens:

Let's say you are intently listening to your love mate and your love mate is momentarily struggling for the right word or idea. If you make the mistake of trying to supply the missing word or idea – even if you're sure you know what it will be – you will immediately derail true listening. Why?

Because you have now forced your love mate to think about *your* word. You have shifted the center of focus from your love mate to *you*. Furthermore, your choice for the missing word will be wrong most of the time.

Likewise, when your love mate says something that strikes a reaction within you, whether favorable or unfavorable, and you jump in to share *your* reaction, you will most probably derail your love mate's heart.

Don't expect to say "I'm sorry" and have your love mate nimbly carry on. Your interruption will break the flow of your love mate moving towards the center of his or her heart. Why? Because, once again, you have shifted the focus to *you* and away from your love mate. People just don't flow from the heart when there are interruptions.

When your love partner comes to a pause and it's not clear whether he or she has more to say, give your love mate the silence that empowers. Here is where the temptation to jump in becomes enormous. Don't! Allow your love mate the joy of experiencing the freedom to relax in patient silence, gather momentum, and go forward.

If you stay tuned to your love mate's heart at exactly this awkward point, your love mate, in the vast majority of cases, will continue launching forward and you will learn what you would have otherwise aborted. You will be amazed at what you have been missing. Your love mate will also be amazed at how much more comes out in your loving presence. You will feel so much closer!

Love
expressed as silent listening says
"I love you"
with liberating force

Reflect Back
What Your Love Mate is
Saying & Feeling

There is a valuable exception to remaining silent while listening. Without some proof from you, how does your love mate know you are honestly and accurately tuned in? In fact, how do *you* know?

The most powerful way to show your love mate that you are tuned in is to reflect back – *occasionally* – what you are hearing. Here's how:

As your love mate is sharing from the heart, ask yourself silently:

> *What is my love mate truly saying and feeling? Can I identify it and convey it so accurately that my love mate would say "Yes!" and continue flowing forward?*

Don't put your love mate's thoughts into your own words or interpretation. Try to reflect back the substance – though not the literal words – of what you are hearing. This is not easy, but it is extremely empowering.

For example, if your love mate has been discussing goals and is obviously pleased with what is coming out, you might add quietly, during a pause:

"I can see you're feeling wonderful about your plans."

Then listen quietly to your love mate's response – both verbal and non verbal.

If your reflecting back is on target and sensitively tuned in to your love mate's heart, he or she will hardly hear you, except perhaps to say *"Yes!"* and then continue sharing even more.

If your reflecting back misses the mark and shows that you are not tuned in, your love mate's sharing will immediately stop and you will sense awkwardness. You will see your love mate's obvious distraction as he or she now attempts to digest or respond to *your* comment.

Don't be discouraged by failures. Most people fail a lot in listening because they are unaware of these powerful listening skills. Practice these skills, however, and you will become an expert listener. You will be amazed at how much you have been missing and you will be deeply valued for your higher love skills.

Counselors and therapists are trained to continuously listen and reflect back what they are hearing. It's no wonder that their clients share from the heart so easily and that so much is revealed for healing. When you do succeed in listening well, you will see with great clarity the empowering effect this has on your love mate and your relationship.

Listen
to your love mate's heart
and watch your love
expand

Chapter 7

Perpetual Intimacy

Love Key #6

Intimacy
unites
us

One afternoon, Shannon gave Scott one of her playful, daring looks, prompting him to chase her down the hallway of our home.

She ran full speed towards our bedroom – and he chased after her. Now, for some reason known only to Shannon, if she can reach and touch our bed before Scott catches her, she yells, *"Safe!"* and she has won.

Well, one day she looked at Scott with that same taunting smile, but he got the jump on her. She was forced to head for the kitchen instead of the bedroom.

"Wait!" she screamed, cornered in the kitchen.

Scott stopped, thinking something unexpected had happened while Shannon raced to grab a pad and pen and furiously began…"What was she doing?" Scott wondered. Has some brilliant new idea struck so hard that she doesn't want to lose it?" Before he could even finish this thought, she screamed with delight:

"Safe!"

She had drawn a tiny picture of our bed – the safe zone – and, with a very victorious smile, was touching the bed (in her drawing) with her finger. Scott had been snookered.

We both had lots of chuckles from that playful little deceit. Needless to say, that ploy only worked once!

Intimacy between love mates occurs at many levels but always flows from a sense of oneness

In genuine love, this sense of oneness is perpetual because both love mates bring so much caring and joy to their love lives.

There are, however, great challenges to perpetual intimacy:

- Our fast paced, instant communication, high demand, stressful world places enormous pressures on relationships. Where do we find time for intimacy?

- Also, after the romance of meeting a love mate, relishing each other's company in courtship, and then settling into an enduring relationship and trying to make ends meet financially, how many relationships maintain a high sense of intimacy?

Yet intimacy is what love is all about. That's why we enter love relationships in the first place.

How can love mates hope to have perpetual intimacy? Here are some ways:

Take Regular Time Off Together

We both have occupations that call on us every day of the week. How can we possibly have a sense of perpetual intimacy?

From the beginning of our marriage, we decided to take Fridays off as our day alone together. Our separate answering machines say, "Hello, this is my day to be with my wonderful partner...."

It's amazing how people respond to this. Our clients not only respect and honor our Fridays together but say, "I should do that too!"

It's not easy to shut down "life" and walk away like this. Think of how tough it is to break loose for a vacation. In a very real sense, we take a mini-vacation every single Friday.

We never quite know what we're going to do on Friday, but we know we will be doing it together – and alone. We never use the day to run errands. It's play day, dream day, think day, share day, pray day, listen day, love day, creative day, quiet day, and movie day all in one.

We often walk on the beach, read and talk at a favorite nature spot, eat lunch overlooking the ocean, and see the latest movie. There are long periods of quiet and free thinking. And lots of bouncing ideas off each other – envisioning, discussing, new revelations, laughter, and inner growth. We also find great support on Fridays for the greatest needs confronting each of us.

What really happens on Fridays is that our hearts connect. It is astounding how much has changed in our lives and thinking in one short week. It is surprising how out-of-tune we are with each other's inner worlds until our hearts have time to unfold in the uninterrupted freedom of our Fridays together.

We connect at the level of each other's desires, fears, doubts, expectations, hopes, and deepest dreams. It is a day of tremendous sorting out, sharing, and healing.

The forces that would interrupt our taking off Fridays together are enormous, but the pattern we have established has created a pathway to intimacy that is too important to miss. It is no wonder that we feel a sense of perpetual intimacy.

This is the intimacy *you* deserve as well!

It doesn't matter whether you are able to take Fridays off together. What matters is that you take time somewhere to be alone and intimate.

Parents, especially, need to make time each week to connect as a couple. Some friends of ours, parents with three young boys, have a standing babysitter every Friday night so they can be together alone.

Actions like this set a great example for kids of what a loving partnership includes – and also helps fulfill the wonderful reasons that led you to make a life together in the first place.

Ask Again (& Again), "What Are You Thinking, Honey?"

This question is so powerful and helpful that it can be sprinkled throughout any day or time together. It brings great clarification and healing to love mates – and instant intimacy.

We ask each other this question frequently. This is not an annoying, prying question when two people love each other. Its real meaning might just as well be phrased:

"Sweetie, I'm sitting here loving you and wondering what's going on in your inner life. If you feel like telling me, I'd love to know. If this isn't a good time, I just want you to know 'I love you.'"

Imagine how good that question feels when you know that this meaning is behind the words.

A big challenge, however, is that the question often catches us emotionally off-guard and may not be easy to answer. We may be deep in private thought – and happy to be there alone – when we hear this question.

But here's what happens in genuine love. Both love mates understand the power behind this question to create intimacy. Both love mates know that the motive behind the question is to stay connected to each other. They knew this is a moment when they are being called – offered an opportunity – to come to the table of intimacy.

And it's not always easy.

Men, for example, may have greater difficulty than women appreciating this question as an opportunity to be intimate:

- It may be that men don't want to reveal what is in their private thoughts – for fear their love mate will disapprove.
- It may be that men are ashamed of what they are thinking.
- It may be that men feel too vulnerable sharing feelings without time to think through what they are thinking.
- It may simply be that men are unaccustomed to sharing in such a way.

Women are much more willing to share feelings and thoughts spontaneously and this freedom of expression strengthens intimacy. Men have a great deal to learn from women on this front.

Understanding this, love mates help each other warm up to the value and benefits of this question and help each other experience success.

They ask the question in a way that conveys great love, joy, and freedom. They do not let their feelings get hurt by a love mate's non-answer, slow answer, or shallow answer.

Let this question enter your love life gently. Create as many opportunities for your love mate to respond in an environment of overwhelming comfort and acceptance. Make sure that each of you walks away feeling glad that you shared – no matter how briefly – in a successful, winning, positive way.

Hold and Touch
Each Other

Intimacy begs for affection and contact.

In the early stages of love, there is great touching, holding of hands, hugging, embracing, kissing, and lovemaking.

What happens once love is established? In many cases, love mates grow distant, separate, and apart. There is less holding and touching.

In genuine love, love mates find perpetual ways to hold and touch each other.

Think how easily you shake hands during the day as you meet person after person. Think how easily you hug a good friend. This is how easily love mates touch and hold and hug and kiss and embrace each other.

Touching, holding, and embracing each other affirms how much you love each other

Touching is contagious. When Shannon's parents came to visit us, we did a lot of walking together as we visited San Diego's many delightful sites.

"Look at those lovebirds," was their early retort as we walked along, often hand-in-hand or arm-in-arm. They poked at our intimacy with humor, but it couldn't be stopped. Our intimacy was just too perpetual. The next day we caught them holding hands too!

In fact, Ed and Sis know a whole lot about intimacy. Married together for over 60 years, and both from small towns in Arkansas, they have been known to stop their car by a familiar country bridge and dance to the music of their car radio.

There are so many levels of intimacy.

Lovemaking is certainly one of them – and a delicate one. Delicate because both love mates need to feel the same desire for lovemaking to be fulfilling. Lovemaking needs to honor *each* love mate, to tune in to the rhythms of each other's needs.

Intimacy calls forth our greatest sensitivities with a love mate. Just look at the chapters in this book that have preceded this discussion of intimacy:

- Loving Yourself
- Friendship First
- Kindness & Honesty Combined
- Cherishing Each Other's Dreams
- Listening To The Heart

These are the building blocks that enable intimacy to flourish. Without this foundation, there will be little touching and holding that satisfies the soul.

Share Your Real Life

Genuine intimacy includes the sharing of what is really going on in your life

Intimacy is more than occasional romance.

Think of your life right now. Think of the vast flow of projects, activities, goals, and tasks that need to be done, and people to talk to, and....

What percent of all this have you shared with your love mate? Does your love mate have any idea what is *really* going on in your life?

It is not easy to unload so much information – even when you want to. It takes time. It takes courage. It takes the right environment. It takes getting past wanting to forget some of it yourself. It takes trusting that your love mate will understand. It takes believing that your love mate wants to know.

Despite all these legitimate concerns, sharing your life openly with your love mate has extraordinary benefits:

- Your love mate will love you even more for your taking the effort to share your world.
- In the very process of trying to awkwardly explain to your love mate your toughest challenge, you will discover solutions you never envisioned.
- You will discover great wisdom and originality in your love mate's responses – because he or she is outside the paradigm of your problem.
- You will find great emotional comfort and satisfaction in sharing what is in your heart, whether happy, challenging, or terrifying.

- You and your love mate will grow more intimate.

Intimacy needs a quiet setting without interruptions. It's a good idea to agree in advance that this time is sacred – no phones or other intrusions. It is also helpful to agree in advance on how much time you both feel will be perfect.

Most men are not too good at sharing their real lives openly. A male colleague told us one day that his wife wanted better communication from him when he came home from work. *"I need more words,"* she told him.

Men, get those words out! Practice revealing your day and thoughts as if a reporter from another planet had just landed in your backyard and was looking to you for insight into an average day on Earth. Learn to give the long version, not the headline. You'll be amazed and delighted at the increased intimacy – and how much you learn and grow within yourself.

Women, don't give up on your love mate. Down deep, men are willing to share their hearts. They just don't have anywhere near the confidence you think they do. Or the practice. Or the commitment to talking. And they don't yet trust in the safety of intimacy. Show them how. Let them feel the benefits. Love them towards this new way of living.

Celebrate Your Love

By the time you read this book, we will have well passed our 100th anniversary – counting by months, naturally! Why wait a year to celebrate the most important person that has ever walked into your life? It's another opportunity to taste the sweet appreciation that fuels perpetual intimacy.

It doesn't matter whether we give each other presents. What matters is that we give each other multiple opportunities to express our love for each other.

For one of Shannon's birthdays, Scott wrote out, in a notebook, 48 reasons why he loved her. He didn't think of this as that great a gift, but it surprised him how much she has treasured it and delighted in sharing it with her parents and our daughter.

When was the last time you told your love mate *why* you loved her or him? Or what you most appreciate about your love mate?

Use the exercise on the next page to open your heart to your love mate, or to a good friend.

The Top 10 Reasons
I Love You

1. _____

2. _____

3. _____

4. _____

5. _____

6. _____

7. _____

8. _____

9. _____

10. _____

When we acknowledge
blessings received from another
our hearts rejoice
in
perpetual intimacy

Chapter 8

Genuine Equality

Love Key #7

Genuine equality is vital to love success.

Inequality in love is devastating – a love-breaker of immense proportions.

Genuine equality in love means that, deep within our private consciousness, we cherish and create the opportunity for our love mate to experience the same depth of joy, opportunity, and quality of love that we expect and cherish for ourselves.

> **Genuine equality**
> **is an inherent,**
> **essential, indisputable, non-negotiable**
> **spiritual right in our love lives**

Genuine equality is bold, clear, and unequivocal. It tells us:

> *"I am honored, treasured, equally important, and equally free to be all that I dream. I am never subordinate to my love mate, and my love mate is never subordinate to me – in any circumstance."*

Envision
Genuine Equality

Envision a relationship of love with genuine equality at its core. If we could look into the internal consciousness of a man or woman experiencing genuine equality in their relationship, what would we see?

We would see each love mate cherishing the other, supporting the other, listening to the other, going to great lengths to ensure that the other was deeply satisfied – in lovemaking, in reaching life dreams, in decision-making, in finances – in every nook of their lives together.

We would see each love mate protecting, defending, promoting, and remembering each other's innate goodness, even during stressful moments – never losing sight of the other's glorious identity.

If we could capture a man's private thoughts on equality, we might hear him thinking to himself:

> *"I love this woman and want her to experience every pleasure that I experience. I want her to experience true equality in our relationship – in our lovemaking, decision-making, reaching for inner dreams, handling of our finances, information sharing, socializing, and in our daily living together.*
>
> *I do not want her to feel a hidden, inner sense of subordination. I do not want generations of masculine domination to obstruct my love mate from experiencing the power of equal importance. And I do not want generations of feminine subordination*

to debilitate her awareness or ability to step into her right to equal importance.

I look forward to loving her in a tender, rich way and having her experience true equality. I look forward to a continuing love exploration with her that will raise us up together in the consciousness and power of equality.

I want to know what she most cherishes in life, what she wants to accomplish, how she honestly feels as we love each other, what she is thinking at her deepest level.

I want her to rise in her true divine self and encourage its complete appearance. I want us both to rejoice in what God has created in her.

Even as I cherish this equality for her, I equally cherish this same equality for myself. I will not allow myself to be treated with any less equality than that which I treasure for her. I am inwardly committed to a relationship that blesses each of us to the maximum, and I know that genuine equality is non-negotiable for this to happen."

**If you are a woman,
think of the above as the inner voice of
the lover you deserve**

If you are a man, compare this to your present consciousness as you think of your love mate.

If we could capture a woman's private thoughts on equality, we might hear her thinking:

"I love this man. I have a vast depth of love to share with him & I want him to feel all of it. I want him to reach for his highest dreams & I am going to love him with every ounce of my being so he feels unburdened, supported, cherished, & happy.

I want to love him so thoroughly that he realizes that he doesn't have to perform in order to be loved. I love him as he is! I want to see even more of his great qualities and name them to him so he can see how I admire and love him. I want his highest Self to be presented to all the world so they can see him as I do, through Love's eyes.

I want to encourage him to grow as much as he wants to and applaud this growth. I want to hold his hand, comfort his fears, understand his heart, and help him realize his dreams.

I want him to know how wonderful he is to the world and how much he means to me, and never take him for granted.

As much as I want all this for him, I also want all this from him – for myself. I want us each to feel the bliss of loving each other with full equality."

**If you are a man,
think of the above as the inner voice of
the lover you deserve**

If you are a woman, compare this to your consciousness as you think of your love mate.

How much of this thinking is real in *your* private heart? Let your heart adopt such thinking as your new love standard.

As we awake to Love's higher possibilities, we are each being called forth to experience the full reality of genuine equality in our love lives. It is your spiritual right, whether you are a woman or a man, to experience equality in every facet of your relationship:

- in the way you are perceived.
- in lovemaking.
- in life path fulfillment.
- in finances.
- in socializing.
- in daily living.

Genuine Equality
In the Way You Are Perceived

We are deeply affected by the way we are perceived by others and, unfortunately for genuine love, there remains deep and terrible injustice throughout the world when comparing women and men.

A woman's substance – worth – is still too often measured as physical by men. And a man's worth is too often measured by what he has accomplished or his financial status.

Although laws have been passed to end discrimination in the workplace, laws cannot penetrate to the inner consciousness that fails to grasp the necessity of genuine, felt-in-the-heart equality.

For men reading this book, suppose that every time you walked into work or a social gathering, you were *primarily* evaluated on how your body looked rather than your individuality, unique talents, and accomplishments. Would this be satisfying?

Of course not! Yet this is the demeaning atmosphere of thought surrounding most women's lives – and it has devastating consequences to a love relationship.

If a man is thinking that a woman's body is her primary substance, he cannot help expressing and communicating this even if no words are spoken. It's as if a man were saying out loud: *"I see you primarily as a body which looks beautiful and sexy -- or a body that doesn't appeal to me."*

This attitude is equally debilitating to genuine love when expressed by a woman towards a man. If he is primarily identified by his physical appeal, his true substance will be missed. Women fixated on finding a "handsome" man are not likely to even be thinking of genuine equality – and unlikely, logically, to then experience it.

In either case, relationships centered foremost on physical attraction play out on the most superficial level. The concept of genuine equality doesn't even appear on the love radar.

Genuine equality just won't happen unless it's way up there on your love list – in your mind and your love mate's.

Of course we want to be physically attracted to our love mate. This is natural and wonderful. But in genuine love, the inner substance of our love mate is honored above all else.

Here's what truly takes place in the love you deserve:

- Love mates recognize that the real substance of their love is not physical but the cherishing of qualities, talents, desires, dreams, goals, and life purpose. They identify and praise each other primarily for their inner values.

- Love mates look at each other as complete equals and cherish their equality. They seek to love each other in exactly the way they would like to be loved themselves.

**We cannot have
rich, satisfying love
without genuine equality**

There is a powerful revolution taking place in our love lives. Love itself is demanding that you be treated with equal importance by your love mate – and that you likewise treat your love mate with genuine equality. This may seem startling but only because it is so missing in our love lives.

We have a long way to go to experience this consciousness of genuine love, but this mental step must be taken to liberate our love lives.

**Cherishing each other's
spiritual right to genuine equality
is a giant step into real love**

Genuine Equality
in Lovemaking

Lovemaking unmistakably reveals the presence – or absence – of genuine equality.

- Whose desires and needs are more important?
- Are both love mates equally open and honest?
- Do both feel equally honored and satisfied?

Without genuine equality, lovemaking is full of performance, dominance, submission, even faked satisfaction. Deep down, no one is truly satisfied.

In genuine love, there is a keen awareness that both partners deserve to experience the fullness of love.

Envision the liberation that would occur if men in lovemaking were not focused on performing, but could enjoy the experience of being truly sensitive to their love mate and relax in their lovemaking?

In genuine love, there is tender, honest communication of each other's desires and this consciousness is devoid of power, dominance, or performance concerns. It is a consciousness that esteems and feels esteemed. No one loses.

Orgasm is not the goal. Experiencing each other at the most intimate level of tenderness, unity, oneness, honoring, and esteem is the ecstasy. This depth of intimacy is unachievable without genuine equality.

Men and women experience satisfaction in different ways, and both partners in genuine love take great joy in meeting each other's needs equally. Is she being encouraged to tell him what gives her the most pleasure? Is he? Are both hearts connecting and speaking love silently through deep, tender regard for each other?

There is great vulnerability in lovemaking. Past treatment, abuse, inability, self-doubt, and lack of trust are powerful negative forces. It is precisely in these most sensitive moments that genuine love is experienced and treasured!

Genuine lovemaking seeks for each partner to feel deeply loved, not just physically, but emotionally. This often calls forth our most needed moments of listening, cherishing, and respecting each other's needs. Here is the potent question:

After lovemaking,
do you feel
cherished, honored, esteemed,
& empowered?

Genuine Equality
in Life Path Fulfillment

As our concept of what is possible in love ascends to higher ground, we find each love mate's life dreams being equally cherished.

Genuine equality
liberates
our creativity

It has traditionally been the woman's role to provide emotional and moral support to a man and his occupation. Today, where it is common for both men and women to have careers, this stereotype is fading, but it is still present. The man's job is still more likely to be considered a "career" and a step along a significant life path where a woman's job is often considered less a part of a significant life path.

Women interrupt or stop their careers to have children, yet, regardless of circumstances, the real issue beneath the surface is whether the woman's life path goals are equally valued. Is her life ever less important than his? No!

Perhaps her choice in life is to be a full-time homemaker and child raiser, at least for a few years. More men, too, are making this choice for themselves.

Just think of the incredible importance of this decision. Is there a higher life path pursuit than raising children in an environment of love, values, and giving them a sense of worth? This is an immense contribution toward furthering peace, eliminating crime, and establishing a better world. Any love mate taking on such an awesome task deserves great honoring and support.

In genuine love, there is a deep desire to enable each love mate to identify and reach for the highest life path dreams. There is an understanding that *life path* is broader and more meaningful than *occupation* and defines our life purpose and the highest use of our talents.

What are her highest dreams? What are his?

These are treasured questions in genuine love, and the answer by each partner is equally treasured.

- Both partners see each other's occupational and life path goals as equally valid and important.
- Both love mates are keenly sensitive to each other's life dreams. They listen to each other repeatedly. They probe to understand. They cherish. They support.

Genuine Equality
in Finances

Money is power.

Inequality on the money front means inequality on the power front. In genuine love, such inequality is unacceptable.

Inequality with finances within a love relationship has disastrous consequences – for women and for men.

For women:

- It is a tragedy that countless women in relationships do not know how much actual money exists in their partnership, where it is, where the complete records are kept, and how to track and manage this money themselves. They are often left out when financial decisions are made. Some may think that they don't need or want to know, but this is likely to catch up with them later.

- It is also a tragedy that too many husbands leave their wives for another woman – often at a point when finally reaching financial success. These wives often don't know how much money exists beyond the household checking account. Small wonder that women suffer so much more financially in a divorce than men.

- It is likewise devastating that many widowed women, who did not participate equally in financial decision-making with their husbands, are exposed to great abuse by those who profit by their unempowered ignorance.

Each instance of such inequality with finances tells a woman that she is not trusted, respected, or able to make such decisions. A women may unconsciously play into this role of unempowerment, but how does this affect her self-worth? How does this affect their love?

Would a man tolerate this with his business partner? Of course not! Why should a love partner put up with such inequality?

Inequality with finances also has terrible consequences for men:

- The tragedy for men is that the practice of not being open with finances unempowers their love mate. Does such a man honestly expect to be richly loved by someone he has stripped of equality? How much love can flow from this condition? How much love is the man sacrificing? A ton!

- The inner loss for men who treat their love mates with financial inequality is even worse. Many men live their entire productive work lives in quiet, nervous desperation, hoping to produce enough income for the family. The deep, inbred belief that it is a man's responsibility to "bring home the bacon" creates enormous guilt and burden. He carries all this alone. This is not Love's way.

A relationship cannot exist at the level of genuine love with such inequality.

Financial equality
empowers our love relationship

In genuine love, there is a deep commitment – by both partners – to empower each other as equals and this is felt at all levels of financial management of their assets, including debt management.

It is a recognition that as each of them understands what is going on with the money, they will both be genuinely empowered and come to mutual, well-discussed decisions together. Each accepts responsibility for financial planning and decisions.

As we were preparing to get married, we had many discussions about money, mostly to get all the information out in the open and help each other be a full participant in the financial planning. This led us to a place of great emotional well-being.

This attitude shifts any burden of financial responsibility from one person to the more powerful shoulders of the partnership. This equal sharing of the burden resolves these needs into joint choices that empower both partners.

It is also deeply empowering when the person who is not the principal income earner is given the opportunity to co-manage and track the finances. The benefit of this is enormous in genuine love. The partner who is not working, or who is bringing in the minority share of income, is empowered by full disclosure of financial information, participation in management, and the learning of valuable skills.

The other love mate is equally empowered by no longer being the only one who truly knows their financial condition – no longer having to carry the burden of financial juggling or decision-making alone.

In genuine love, both love mates have open discussions to decide budget issues, options, priorities, and financial strategies. They act as a support and comfort to each other, lifting each other's load.

Genuine love includes a commitment and joy in full financial disclosure, completely open financial records, and great sensitivity to not overspending without mutual consent.

Each partner wants the other to experience genuine financial equality and sees financial dealings as another way to demonstrate their great love for each other.

Genuine Equality
in Socializing

Socializing with others is another area of life where genuine equality is deeply needed for true love to flourish.

When you are in a social setting with other love partners, how long does it take to determine whether two people love each other with equality? About three seconds. The evidence of inequality is instantly obvious:

- How often does one partner put down the other, either openly, or with subtle looks and behaviors?
- Is a woman judged by her looks or by her inner substance? How is a man being judged?
- Are each love mate's thoughts and opinions on issues valued equally?
- Is each partner aware when the other partner is being put down by another?
- Does a love mate allow a humiliating or offensive remark to pass for social reasons?

In genuine love, there is alert sensitivity to valuing each partner's contribution and expression of ideas. And there is alert sensitivity to the way a love partner is being treated by others.

For example, an offensive joke that puts down women is not ignored simply to be socially polite.

Would we allow our children or our mothers to be put down? No! Is your love mate less important?

Poor taste or abuse in humor is graciously addressed rather than politely ignored. Why should "friends" be allowed to attack the very fabric of your love relationship – even indirectly? The impact of inequality in social circles is demeaning and comes directly home with you and your love mate once you leave the party.

Here's another example. Some partners show blatant interest in other men or women – right in front of their love mates. This attitude, even if an unconscious or a social habit, is utterly demeaning to a love mate. Many love partners let this go unchallenged because they are accustomed to abuse, even if mild. *"Oh that's just the way he (or she) is."*

It's time for this to cease.

Wake up men!

Wake up women!

Here, again, is the potent test. Next time you are in a social gathering with your love mate, stop at random and ask yourself privately:

Do I feel honored, valued, empowered?
Does my love mate?

Genuine Equality
in Daily Living

Genuine equality doesn't vacillate. It's a cherishing that is pervasive in every aspect of your daily life with your love mate. Real equality between love mates is so genuine that it sneaks into the smallest portions of our daily lives.

We both laugh at ourselves in the way we almost compete for who will be first to drag out the garbage cans, bring in the groceries, clean up after a meal, or provide that small touch of love that brings a smile to the inner heart.

Envision multiplying this attitude to every task that confronts a loving couple. It is immensely empowering. It lubricates the foundation of the love relationship. It is as if you say to each other a thousand times each day:

> *"I love living with you. I want to make your life a joy! I want to ease your load as much as possible. I want us to relish living together."*

Genuine equality is not measured by whether each does half of each routine. Shannon does most of the cooking and shopping in our daily routine. Scott is not completely comfortable with this because a woman's traditional role of cooking is so often unappreciated, so he is sensitive to any signs that she would rather eat out or have him cook (the first being the more tasty option). We eat out a lot!

Scott is also sensitive to the fact that the person cooking can easily get the idea that he or she is subservient in the relationship. So he makes sure that Shannon feels appreciated. He doesn't sink into an attitude of expecting service.

Take another routine in a love relationship – driving. Both love mates jump in the car to go somewhere, anywhere. Who's the driver? Was there a discussion? Does each get equal opportunity? Do you know your partner's preference?

Shannon *loves* to drive and Scott cherishes her opportunity to be in command in the traditionally male-dominated driver's seat. Yet even as Shannon feels the joy of this freedom and equality, she is always asking, with a twinkle, "Are you sure you wouldn't like to drive?" And often Scott does. It's a wonderful example of each of us receiving what we need because our hearts are so in touch.

Each tiny moment of routine life adds up to a delicious experience of equality – or an overwhelming sense of inequality.

- Who drives?
- Who gets the most comfortable chair?
- Who decides which movie to see?
- Who decides what car to buy?
- Who takes out the garbage?
- Who cleans up?
- Who controls the remote control?

In genuine love,
there is nothing too small or routine
to be valued
through the lens of equality

Chapter 9

Empowering Manhood

Love Key #8

Manhood is undergoing a massive yet almost invisible – revolution.

Most men, of course, don't talk. That's why this revolution is so invisible. Almost alone, without much support, men are grappling with what it means to be "a man" as we move towards a new civilization that is screaming for manhood's consciousness to open up.

Two radically different roads are being presented to men in the privacy of their own consciousness.

The old road – "Power man" – calls men down the centuries-old path of manhood as the power master of the universe. Man the provider. Man the decision-maker. Man the protector. Man the leader.

The new road – "Empowering man" – calls men forth into an emerging world that is being created right now. Man an empowerer. Man a nurturer. Man a creator of equality. Man a healer.

On the planet as a whole, unfortunately, only a fraction of men are even aware of these choices. To the misery of themselves and those around them, many men live out their internal and external lives completely trapped in the "Power man" paradigm.

They are so wrapped up in controlling, dominating, and making decisions for others that they are blind to the consequences – blind, really, to their way of living. The consequences for these men in intimate love relationships are devastating.

An increasing number of men, however, are awakening to the second path. These men are carving out a new definition of "real manhood" – but they are doing so without a clear model in mind and without a strong, visible support system that applauds their progress.

Men desperately need a vision of who they are and the great worth they have to contribute to a world progressing at almost breath-taking speed technologically, and turtle-speed in intimate relationships.

We are on the edge of an historical shift in the meaning of manhood

We need a vision of manhood that can equal the significance of our civilization's awakening. We also need a vision that can open the door for men to an intimate love life that far exceeds their current experience. This vision can be summarized in one potent phrase:

Empowering man!

To understand the vision of man as an empowerer, we must first understand why manhood has been trapped – forever, it seems – in the paradigm of "Power man."

An Intimate Look at "Power Man"

For the vast majority of males on Earth, here's what it's been like to grow up "like a man."

Men are socialized to believe in winning

From earliest childhood, boys are expected to win, not lose – whether in baseball, basketball, football, soccer, track, tennis, or a neighborhood game of tag. A man's self-worth goes up with winning, down with losing. Even adult men watching a sports event on TV take sides. They want their side or player to win.

Men are socialized to believe in strength

From their earliest years, boys are expected to be strong. A young man works to develop strength to win in sports. A young man measures his self worth by the extent of his physical strength.

A man is handed the jar when the top won't give way. A man is expected to move heavy furniture without complaint. Manhood is strength. To lack strength is to lack manhood.

Men are socialized to believe that they are protectors

Young men are expected to protect their sisters or younger brothers. A young man is also expected to protect himself from bullies or enemies, whether he has the skills or not.

An adult man is expected to protect his family. A man is also expected to protect his nation from any and all enemies. Men learn that to protect requires the power to dominate – or at least appear to dominate.

Men are socialized to believe that they are providers

Young men know, from an early age, that they will be responsible for providing what is needed to sustain a family.

College, vocational training, and work experiences are known in the heart to be preparation for the real job of being a provider. Every work and learning experience is part of the trial of manhood, proving or disproving his capacity to provide.

It doesn't matter that a woman today provides a share, or even a majority, of what is needed. It is still embedded in consciousness, as part of Power man's identity, that it is a man's responsibility to provide.

Men are socialized to believe that money is power

Men learn at an early age that it takes money to provide, to protect, to win.

Money is the resource that opens doors. Men see that those with money have power. Men must make money because power is needed to fulfill the obligations of being a man. Making money says to a man that he is worthy.

Men are socialized to believe that they can control any situation

From developing a play on the football field to developing a battle plan that will defeat the enemy, men think in terms of control.

Power men believe it is their role in life to control since control is needed to protect and provide. Man measures his self-worth by the extent that he is in control of his environment and those around him.

Men are socialized to believe that women are inferior

It can't be too much of a surprise, by this point, to understand why Power man would perceive women as inferior. Power man thinks.

- Women are not as strong.
- Women should not be the providers.
- They don't protect.
- They can't control.
- They don't know how to win.
- They often don't even want to win.
- They don't understand the importance of power.

What then happens when this "Power man" comes face-to-face with intimate love?

The Impotence & Danger
of Power Man in Intimate Love

Intimate love thrives on tenderness, sharing, giving, feeling – not controlling, dominating, speed, and power.

Power man isn't trained for this. In fact, Power man goes ballistic even thinking of giving up control or power to anyone, even his love mate. Wouldn't that be weakness? Wouldn't that make him vulnerable? What would be his worth?

It isn't that Power man doesn't want love. It's that love has a different meaning to him. A true love mate, he reasons, would look up to him, revere his strength, and allow him to remain in control to fulfill his destiny of manhood.

When it comes to sexual interaction, Power man is clear cut. The object of sex is not caressing, closeness, and a sharing of intimacy, but culmination. Climax is touchdown! Did he win? Did he provide? Did he satisfy himself?

This attitude does not lead to a deepening of intimate love, to mutual satisfaction, or to increasing sensitivity to each other's needs.

It is easy to laugh at Power man's attempts to forge an intimate love relationship, but men are, indeed, stumbling towards a new definition of manhood – a new manhood that is able to successfully create and support intimate love.

But for those Power men who have no plans to change, there is both frustration and danger. Convinced of his ability to control and the necessity of exercising power over his environment, he is a real threat to women – and himself.

He considers it his choice to do with women what he wishes. He has power. He is trained to control, to dominate, to win.

Even as we look out on a broad Earth-scale view of world consciousness, we see that the raping of women, for example, has been widely accepted as simply a part of life – in war and peace. Only recently has rape been classified as a crime in war.

The immense tragedy of the Power man mentality still rampant in civilization today begs for transformation. Our intimate love lives are being tragically short-changed. Our entire world desperately needs a solution – for both men and women.

We need a vision of manhood that can uplift, not destroy, a vision of manhood as empowering, not dominating.

Civilization's New Manhood
"Empowering Man"

Thousands of men are already making the journey from Power man to the expanded and richer experience of Empowering man:

- These men have learned to loosen up, to share their feelings, to talk more openly with other men and woman, to value the significant contribution their partners are making as providers.
- These men are highly respectful and honoring of women.
- These men have outgrown, or are outgrowing, the sense of separation between a man's world and a woman's world.
- These men value their own femininity, though they might refer to it as a greater

appreciation for tenderness and nurturing combined with their strength.

- These men are more deeply involved in raising their kids with qualities of mothering as well as fathering.
- These men are having more satisfying intimate love experiences. They are sharing feelings more openly with their love mates. They are discovering the benefits of intimate love that is mutually satisfying and uplifting.

Even these men, however, are still wrestling with the two worlds – the old Power man who looks increasingly out-of-touch with today's reality and the new, softer man seeking to harmonize with a world of active, intelligent, contributing women. This new Empowering man is seeking, in fact, to harmonize with himself and his growing appreciation of a more emotionally-open existence.

This transition is not easy, even for more liberated men. A steady flow of daily circumstances – at work, in society, in sports, and in private conversations with other men – block the transition to new manhood. Some men banter politely with the Power men they encounter. Some men are more and more repulsed. Others have begun to speak up.

This is the seeding of the revolution in manhood that is ready to bloom in our awakening world. The shift will have gigantic consequences.

**We are witnessing the emergence
of man as an empowerer**

What it Means
to Empower

To empower means to create an environment for another person to feel, experience, and acquire the full benefits of the power you already possess.

When a coach shows a young man (or woman) the secret of how to correctly execute a play, that is an empowering act. It is empowering because the student, with practice, now has the opportunity to execute that play just as well as the coach.

When a master carpenter teaches a student the secrets of the trade, that is an empowering act. It enables that student to duplicate, and with practice, even excel, the master.

When someone teaches you how to send e-mail, how to create a web page on the internet, or how to use a computer program, that is an empowering act – because now you can do it too.

Teams are also empowering. Any truly successful sports team, hostage-rescue team, or business team understands the necessity of combining talents and teaching each other the skills necessary for success.

Anyone who has participated in a winning team also understands the exhilaration of drawing on each other's strengths to create a flow towards victory. Successful teams depend on their individual members to empower each other and to teach each other the skills and secrets that will enable them all to perform at a level of grace and excellence.

When it comes to serious power, however, we are less likely to share our knowledge with others. We are fearful that if others learn our secrets, they could displace us, defeat us, or make us vulnerable. This is true in war, in business, and in love. That is why:

To empower another is a courageous act of vision & love

It is **courageous** because an empowerer, rather than seeking to protect or retain power, creates the opportunity for another person to gain, possess, and utilize power.

It takes **vision** because an empowerer, rather than fearing loss of power, sees that bringing others into equal power enhances life, business, and love – for the empowerer as well.

It takes **love** because an empowerer looks at the other as deeply worthy of experiencing and enjoying all that the empowerer experiences and enjoys, rather than defining another as a potential enemy who must be blocked from gaining power.

The Benefits of Being An Empowerer

The benefits of being an empowerer are enormous:

- By teaching another our skills, we refine with greater clarity what we know, or think we know. We become better ourselves.
- By empowering another, we see the enormous increase in the other's self-worth – all from something very easy for us to do.
- By empowering another, we discover that we can, ourselves, more easily tackle the problems we have been facing alone. We become team-builders. The burden of being the only one responsible for solutions flows to the team we ourselves help to forge and

empower. Envision the power and joy of such teamwork with your love mate!

- By empowering another, we show our children the meaning of true manhood.
- By empowering another, our own self-worth skyrockets – because we are far more richly honored as an Empowering man than as a Power man. We begin to see the incredible impact of our true power as empowerers.

***Empowering man
becomes an admired hero
who represents true manhood***

The Potency of Empowering Man In Intimate Love

When a man becomes an empowerer in his intimate love life, the benefits are extraordinary – to both love mates. By seeking to empower his love mate:

- He communicates that he wants his love mate to enjoy all the benefits of life that he enjoys.
- He discovers the immense satisfaction of enabling his love mate to gain skills and power that he has learned or acquired.
- His love mate feels the strength and depth of his love and sharing and is far more likely to empower back with her own skills and experience.

- He releases the burden of thinking that he alone is responsible for providing and protecting.
- The bond between love mates is forged at a higher, more mutually-satisfying level of equality.
- He discovers the joy of contributing all that he has learned and gained from manhood with his love mate.

Becoming an empowerer
of your love mate
raises your love life to a phenomenal
new dimension

Here are easy steps that will help you become an expert empowerer:

Decide to Be An Empowerer

It is not difficult to become an empowerer once you make the decision.

The key is your motivation.

If your motivation is primarily to impress your love mate with your skills, you will fall short. An Empowering man seeks to have his love mate impressed by what *she* can do as a result of his empowering.

If your motivation is simply to have a higher sense of worth yourself, you will also fall short. The higher goal is to enable *your love mate* to have a higher sense of worth.

If your motivation is to truly enable your love mate to understand, practice, and master whatever power you have to share, your love mate will feel the underlying genuineness of your motivation and your empowering will be successful.

An Empowering man looks for ways he can empower his love mate.

***Liberation,
not domination
is the goal of Empowering man
in genuine love***

Identify Who Has Most Empowered You & How?

Who are the top people in your whole life who have most empowered you?

- _____
- _____
- _____
- _____
- _____

What are the most significant things these people did to empower you?

- _____
- _____
- _____
- _____
- _____

Let these skills be your model as you move towards empowering expertise.

Identify Ways You Can Empower Your Love Mate

Now that you are thinking of yourself as an empowerer, ask yourself:

- What power do I most prize in my own life?
- Does my love mate have this power?
- What other information or skills do I have that would most benefit my love mate?
- What power – information, knowledge, or skills – does my love mate most desire?

If you don't know, ask your love mate. You might be surprised by her answers. Even if you think you know, ask. You'll still be surprised!

***An empowerer
is constantly looking for ways
to empower his
love mate***

Start Empowering

Start practicing, with your love mate, the skills you have learned from thinking of those who have empowered your life.

For example, when we first married, Shannon had little computer experience. Scott loves computers and his professional experience has given him wide expertise with many computer programs. Here, he realized, was a wonderful opportunity to share what he had learned with Shannon. His goal was to help *her* become an expert, not to do work for her.

It wasn't without a struggle. When Shannon would reach a point of *"I can't take any more learning right now,"* we laughed (most of the time) and stopped. But she knew Scott was there as a resource, that he would not withhold secrets, and that she could draw on his expertise at her convenience. That itself was empowering. Today, she is independently competent with her computer.

And our empowering has been reciprocal. Rather than thinking we each have separate skills and that's just the way it is, we seek to empower each other so we can both have extended skills.

For example, Shannon has helped Scott learn and refine his skills as a spiritual healer. This is something Scott wasn't even sure he was capable of, yet today it is a natural part of his identity. In fact, he is the healer Shannon turns to when she is in need.

Imagine the depth of joy and intimacy this has created in our marriage!

Here's another excellent way to tune in to your love mate's needs and be an empowerer. Ask your love mate: *"On a scale of 1 to 10, to what extent do you feel empowered by me?"*

The mere asking of this question – if genuine – is empowering to a love mate.

If your love mate says "8," don't breathe a sigh of relief and go back to your own world. Ask the key follow-up question, *"What would make it a 10?"* Now you'll get some real answers. You may not always like them, but remember, your goal isn't to feel self satisfied but for your love mate to feel empowered. This exercise is about your love mate's well-being, not yours.

Be prepared to be surprised by what your love mate truly desires. You may be providing a car, income for maintaining the family, and a whole lot more, but your love mate may want something as simple as being treated as an equal decision maker.

Another way to learn about empowering is to put yourself in the role of the one being empowered. Ask your love mate to teach you something that you truly want to learn. What power, knowledge, or skills do you most wish you could have from your love mate? Ask your love mate to empower you in this area.

Just this asking, if honest, will empower your love mate because it says that you find your love mate highly valuable to you.

By letting your love mate empower you, you will also learn how it feels to be the one empowered. It often feels awkward, frustrating, and debilitating to be the one being empowered because the spotlight is on our weakness. Learn from this how to be a better, clearer, more patient empowerer yourself.

Practice Empowering in Lovemaking

Lovemaking calls forth the highest skills of empowering – listening, tuning in, connecting, and being at one with each other.

What does your love mate truly want – gratification, caressing, or perhaps just close emotional time together? Real lovemaking is not a momentary act disconnected from the rest of your relationship. Are your love actions based on meeting your needs or on empowering your love mate?

To truly empower your love mate, tune in to your partner's desires, needs, feelings, fears, concerns, and hopes. Discuss these openly – and be ready to learn a lot about your love mate's inner heart.

Chapter 10

Empowered Womanhood

Love Key #9

Womanhood is at the leading edge of a Great Awakening in our civilization.

While men are grappling with the transition from Power man to Empowering man, women are simultaneously moving towards a redefinition of their highest identity as we catapult into a new era of infinite opportunities.

> *The great challenge to civilization
> today is to
> fully empower Womanhood*

There is enormous resistance to the full empowerment of womanhood:

- Civilization for centuries has placed womanhood in second place.
- Most men are not yet advanced enough in their consciousness to encourage fully empowered womanhood.
- Because of her own dedication to empowering *others,* a woman's dreams, needs, and ambitions are often put on hold, relegated to second place, or ignored – even by herself.
- Women are torn between conflicting roles of mothering & professional development.

This combined consciousness adds up to an enormous wall of resistance to empowered womanhood – but this wall is crumbling.

The very core of womanhood is her nurturing expertise – her ability to enable *others* to succeed. Empowering others is as natural to most women as exercising power is to most men. The immense need now for womanhood is to turn her nurturing expertise inward and empower *herself.*

Why
should women,
who comprise 51% of the Earth's population,
live at a lower level of
honoring, dignity, worth, opportunity,
power & love
than men?

A New Level of Awareness of Womanhood's Immense Value

Here is a potent question that breaks through the crust of accumulated thinking about womanhood and magnifies her immense value:

What would our civilization be like
if women did not exist?

- Where would our children turn for mothering?
- Who would teach our children?
- Would there be any children?

- Where would we find warmth, praise, encouragement, and nurturing for our dreams?

- How would we fill the vacuum of the loss of a woman's love?

- Where would we find the lost insight & intuition that women bring to the issues that confront our lives and civilization?

- Where would we be without the women who comprise 51% of the population on our planet?

- Where would we be without the talented women leaders who have been named to the National Women's Hall of Fame in the United States? They include: Bella Abzug, Madeleine Albright, Maya Angelou, Susan B. Anthony, Clara Barton, Rosalynn Carter, Emily Dickenson, Amelia Earhart, Mary Baker Eddy, Ella Fitzgerald. Betty Friedan, Barbara Jordan, Helen Keller, Anne Morrow Lindbergh, Dr. Shannon Lucid, Margaret Mead, Sandra Day O'Connor, Georgia O'Keeffe, Rosa Parks, Sally Ride, Eleanor Roosevelt, Elizabeth Cady Stanton, Gloria Steinem, Harriet Beecher Stowe, Sojourner Truth, Oprah Winfrey and many more that have deeply advanced our civilization.

- How many more women of great value can you name?

Is your appreciation of womanhood expanding? Let us envision what will happen when civilization lets loose the chains of mental subordination and supports Empowered womanhood.

The issue is not whether womanhood is more valuable than manhood but equally valuable

Empowered Womanhood
Will be Cherished
for Her Infinite Spiritual Love

True womanhood expresses the beauty, ability, strength, intelligence, and brilliance of Love. This is the true essence of womanhood, the basis from which her lovely radiance pours forth.

As women see themselves as the spiritual expression of divine, infinite Love, they will feel the enormous power of their healing identity

As men, too, come to see women as the embodiment of this highest Power, they will grow in their admiration and support of Empowered womanhood and also recognize these wonderful qualities in themselves. Imagine living in a world where women as well as men rise to the height of their genuine essence and worth.

Empowered Womanhood
will Shape the New Civilization

All civilization feels the immense power of a woman's nurturing expertise.

An ideal mother's love, for example, is unconditional. It sticks by us even when we stray. It never casts us off. It remains and loves us. It calms, soothes, praises, encourages, and blesses. It remembers our innate goodness and reminds us of it.

This nurturing is a great force – a massive power in our lives – and it is now being called forth to uplift our entire civilization.

***The time has come
for women to become nurturers
not just for their offspring or love mates,
but for themselves &
the entire world***

The Earth's people are emotionally starving – silently and audibly crying to be lifted out of repression, fear, starvation, domination, and abuse and lifted into a nurturing, caring, honoring, empowering environment. In other words, civilization desperately needs Empowered Womanhood.

***Our world
needs women
as consciousness leaders
& models***

Women intuitively know what our world needs. Women *have* the consciousness and skills of empowering others that can bring harmony to centuries of entrenched hatred, fear, abuse, and rebellion. Our entire civilization is in great need of the unleashed strength of Empowered womanhood.

As women come to see themselves in the brilliant Light of empowered identity and *exercise* their full womanhood, everyone will benefit:

- Women will feel the joy and satisfaction of seeing their true identity honored and utilized – without restriction.
- Men will see worldwide problems dissolving under the healing influence of womanhood's love, intuition, and empowering strength.

- Our planetary home will become a stronger, safer, more compassionate environment for us all.
- Women and men will enter into love partnerships with equal support to each other.

Empowered Womanhood
Will Provide Spiritual Vision

Our civilization is hungering for womanhood's spiritual vision and guidance – and it is coming forward. We see Empowered womanhood's spiritual vision more evident today than ever in governments, organizations, churches, communities, families, and intimate relationships.

Consciousness is awakening to the great contribution of womanhood to our well-being as a civilization. Men are also cherishing womanhood's great spiritual healing power and welcoming it into their lives.

The moment in history
has arrived for Empowered womanhood
to rise to the full consciousness
of her immense worth
and exercise with authority
her spiritual talents

Empowered Women
Will Experience Far Richer
Love Lives

As a woman lives her life from the consciousness of Empowered womanhood and cherishes her spiritual authority and immense value to civilization, her love life will expand into the glory it deserves!

Imagine the benefits that an Empowered woman brings to intimate love:

- She feels the freedom of being able to make her own choices free of fear, domination, or control by a man.
- She does not fall for a love mate who will hold her back from her life mission.
- She exudes confidence and strength.
- She loves and admires herself for being true to herself and expressing her identity fully and well.
- Her self worth is at a *sustained* high.
- She will not allow herself to be undermined.
- She is an expert at empowering herself and feels the powerful strength this brings to her identity and love life.

Enlightened men today are seeking empowered and self-honoring women. And yes, women, these men exist. To accept less from a man will erode your true identity. Any man who does not honor Empowered womanhood will do nothing but hold back your life from it's highest fulfillment.

How is the vision of Empowered womanhood going to happen in your life? Here are some bold steps you can take as a woman – and support as a man:

Decide to Be
An Empowered Woman

This is not as obvious a decision as you might think.

- Some women may say "Yes" to being an Empowered woman but still want the advantages of being protected and provided for, even if this means being subordinate.
- Many women are still unaccustomed to equal power. Being empowered moves the balance of power towards equality and this shift transforms almost every facet of an intimate love relationship.

Where do *you* stand – internally – in the great awakening of Empowered womanhood? You have the freedom and choice to raise your love life to a level that honors Empowered womanhood, but will you do it?

Here's a test situation. Let's say you identified the top 10 qualities you are looking for in a love partner and "an Empowering man who honors Empowered womanhood" is one of the 10 requirements. Now suppose a very appealing man comes along who scores 7 out of 10 on your love list. He is handsome, fun, talented, wealthy, but, unfortunately, honoring womanhood is not on his agenda.

Would you say to yourself: "Go for it, seven out of ten is not that bad. I may never get more."

Or would you say to yourself:

Nothing
is going to prevent me
from experiencing an Empowering man
who honors Empowered womanhood!
I will not settle for less!

The big question is not, "Are you willing to lose the man?" The defining question is, "Are you willing to give up your life as an Empowered woman?"

Imagine yourself rising to the level of self-honoring where you could say to this potential love mate:

> *"There is a whole lot that appeals to me about you, but I'm not willing to settle for a man who does not know how to honor Empowered womanhood or have an equally empowering relationship."*

Your inner commitment to the love you deserve sends out a message to the entire universe. And the universe will respond. That may seem an outrageously bold statement, but it is a true statement.

This is part of your love education – to recognize that the values you treasure in your private heart will exude from your being. All those around you – including men who are empowerers – will feel your strength and be drawn to your higher sense of identity.

**If you are
committed to an
empowering love relationship,
you will experience it**

Identify Your Highest Value
As A Woman

How would you define *your* highest value as an Empowered woman?

Think about this carefully. What would give you the greatest possible sense of life fulfillment as an Empowered woman?

- _____

- _____

- _____

- _____

- _____

This is the
Empowered woman within you
to protect, support, nurture, liberate,
empower, express,
& fully love

Choose a Love Partner
Who Will Support Your
Highest Identity

We so much want to be loved that we are tempted to settle for less than we deserve.

Your true womanhood, however, is bringing you into deep spiritual alignment with Love at a level of satisfaction and bliss beyond what you can yourself ordain.

Your Empowered womanhood is not a weakness or liability. It is an immense Light of irresistible spiritual charm. This is exactly the quality of woman that an Empowering man is seeking within his heart. As we discuss in the upcoming chapter, *Finding the Love Mate of Your Dreams,* give yourself the joy of meeting your love mate in the Light.

You will never lose real love by taking this empowered position. Too much is at stake for you to settle for a love mate who is not an empowerer. You have moved so beautifully and thoroughly into Light that your true identity can no longer accept a relationship of control, manipulation, domination, games, or abuse. This is all behind you now because your consciousness is awake.

The love mate you deserve
seeks, cherishes, honors, & delights
in an Empowered woman

Put *Your* Life in First Place

This can be a very challenging step for a woman, or for a man to support, since it is history's legacy for a woman to support her man, to support her children, and to wait for her turn. Hence:

Womanhood needs to
exaggerate putting her life
in first place
even to approximate balance
with a man

It is not selfish for you to put your life in first place. This does not mean abandoning your partner, parents, children, or their needs. What it does mean is not abandoning *you!* Take responsibility for keeping your needs equally met.

Be The Empowered Woman You Admire

Think of the women in history or that you know today that you most admire. What qualities do they have in common?

- _____
- _____
- _____
- _____
- _____

Let this standard of Empowered womanhood flow into your identity and life practice.

Love Yourself as An Empowered Woman

Let your new sense of identity as a confident, Empowered woman exude from your consciousness and life activities. Practice *living* in the high consciousness of true womanhood. Practice *loving* in this consciousness.

***Fall in love with yourself
as an Empowered
woman***

When you think of attracting a love mate – or even more fully attracting your present love partner – are you *waiting* to be appreciated, loved, valued, and wanted? True womanhood abandons this unempowering status of waiting for a prince to recognize her beauty and rescue her.

This is the consciousness of womanhood in genuine love. She knows her worth. She knows her intrinsic beauty. She loves her life. She loves herself.

No one can hand this gift to you. As womanhood perceives that she *has* this spiritual radiance, it will exude from her life with grace and authority.

You are already
beautiful & complete as
Love's radiance

Chapter 11

Loving Out
From Spirituality

Love Key #10

Spirituality is the golden key that opens genuine love to infinite possibilities and bliss.

The essence of spirituality is the understanding that a Higher Power has created us and is expressing each of us. We are one with a divine Source. This great spiritual truth illumines why genuine love is possible:

***Genuine love is possible
for each of us
because Love is the infinite Source
of all the love
we give & receive***

We do not create love. Love creates and expresses us. We are not acquiring love. We are discovering love. We are not climbing *towards* love. We are living *out from* Love. In short:

***We are not becoming spiritual
We are spiritual***

Once we enter this consciousness of spiritual Love, our love lives come into clear focus and dramatically expand:

- We redefine ourselves as purely spiritual, hence purely loving.
- We see our love mate as spiritual and the expression of spiritual Love.
- We see our love relationship as a spiritual event and Love union.
- We open our hearts and minds to the infinite embrace and possibilities of Love.

We all feel the energy of this spiritual awakening. More and more, we are looking within for spiritual answers. We are reading books on spirituality, meditating privately, and discovering our spirituality in our own way. And whatever our path, we are all arriving at the same place in consciousness – our oneness with Love.

Spirituality
is our core substance

Spirituality is no longer a *portion* of our identity or something we tack on to our love relationships. Spirituality *is* our *complete* identity and the *main* ingredient of genuine love.

This revelation is as paradigm-shattering as Einstein's consciousness which changed the way we perceived our universe. The universe did not change with Einstein. Our *consciousness* changed and that changed our world. Today, the paradigm-shattering revolution taking place in consciousness is our understanding of spirituality and oneness in Love.

It may seem that some of us have spirituality in our love lives and some of us do not, but this is a mistaken view.

Spirituality
is the central principle
of our love lives whether we see it or not

All the love you have ever known or ever will know is already within you. You *already include* this love – and it all flows from Love Itself. Spirituality is the substance of all the love you will ever experience – forever – with anyone.

If we are ignorant of spirituality, this does not make the spiritual nature of our being less true. Ignorance only hides spirituality from our view and experience. We are all living at different stages of *discovering* spiritual Love as our inherent identity and this has wonderful consequences for our love lives.

Awareness
of our spirituality
enables us to experience the
infinite nature of all-embracing Love

Become aware of spirituality as the force of Love guiding your love life to fulfillment. Here are some ways that will enable you to see your love life in its spiritual light:

See The
10 Keys to Genuine Love
as Spiritual Love In Action

With the view of spirituality *as* Love, think again of what you have read so far in this book. Each of the 10 keys to genuine love shows a tangible way of expressing the nature and power of spiritual Love.

- **Loving Yourself** acknowledges your true identity as the expression of Love.
- **Friendship First** creates a bond of pure, spiritual unity.
- **Kindness & Honesty Combined** express the unity and power of Love and Truth in simultaneous action.
- **Cherishing Each Other's Dreams** demonstrates the infinite, complete, and honoring nature of divine Love.
- **Listening to the Heart** is spiritual Love in action at the highest level of cherishing.
- **Perpetual Intimacy** demonstrates the delight of Spirit flowing through our love union.
- **Genuine Equality** upholds the co-equal status of our spiritual identity and worth.
- **Empowering Manhood** acknowledges the true spiritual nature of men as ambassadors of all-empowering Love.
- **Empowered Womanhood** acknowledges the freedom, worth, and completeness of women in the eyes of divine Love.
- **Loving Out From Spirituality** unites us with our true identity – living and loving in Love.

See Identity as Spiritual, Not Physical

What are the best love relationships you have ever observed and what made them so good?

1. _____
2. _____
3. _____
4. _____
5. _____

Outside our own beautiful marriage, we each think of the sweet relationships of our parents. Their love included:

1. Consistent kindness
2. Unconditional love
3. Dedication to spirituality
4. Joy and humor
5. Embracing others with open love

Notice what you are *not* hearing – height, weight, looks, education, or financial status. That would give no clue whatsoever to why these relationships succeeded.

**By seeing
real identity as spiritual, not physical,
we see with the eyes of Love**

How about your description of the most successful relationship you know? Did you describe spiritual qualities or physical assets and appearance?

Now let's take this exercise another step forward and uncover *your* true identity. Remember:

Who you are &
what you truly bring
to a relationship
is spiritual

Describe your spiritual identity in five words or phrases. Don't be shy. We're talking about the very essence within you that will establish genuine love in your life:

1. _____

2. _____

3. _____

4. _____

5. _____

Your spiritual identity
is what makes you irresistibly
attractive & loveable

Love Out
From Spirituality

The summit of spiritual consciousness is to recognize that love is not outside you, but within you. Love created you, is within you, and is expressing you right now. You are at one with Love. This awareness of your true identity as a Love being puts your life in the beautiful position of loving out from spirituality. Love is radiating you!

To love out from Love rather than struggling to find Love enables you to drop guilt, fear, doubt, and low self-worth and adopt a consciousness that knows how beautiful and valuable you are as Love's radiance. Envision yourself loving out from Love and thinking:

I feel Love's presence and power
as my very own nature and expression
Love is expressing Itself
to the world as me

To feel such oneness with Love is radically empowering – to ourselves and to our love mates. If you are presently without a love mate, such oneness with Love causes love to flow into your life with infinite abundance. Here is the beautiful, spiritual truth about you:

- You are Love's very own nature – incapable of expressing anything less than genuine Love.
- You are Love's recipient – destined to experience Love's infinite treasures.
- You are Love's outpour – showing your love mate and all others in your life what Love feels like through your thoughts and actions.

If you catch yourself saying, "I don't think I can do all that," then turn to divine Love and lean. Ask for inspiration and guidance. Listen while Love shows you the way. Open yourself to your inherent unity with Love and let Love express Itself profusely and infinitely *as* you.

Even now,
this precious moment,
divine Love is cherishing you,
expressing you, & guiding you into
all the love you so
richly deserve

Chapter 12

Finding the Love Mate of Your Dreams

Finding the love mate of your dreams is not only possible, it is what Love wants for you.

The desire to be genuinely loved is natural and right – and this desire will be fulfilled as you open your heart to the love you deserve.

As you read this chapter, please remember how immensely valuable you are. You have vast gifts of love to share and oceans of love to receive. Love Itself is inviting you to open your heart, mind, and spirit to a change of view of what is possible to Love. Think beyond *hope*. Think beyond *dream*. Think beyond *perhaps*.

Think *spiritual right*.

It is your spiritual right to experience a*ll* of Love. This is the love you deserve.

**Love comes
to each of us differently
but always in Love's perfect way**

Why then does finding love seem so hard?

Because the world's view of love creates so much love fog. Let us walk together beyond the fog into Love's Light where finding the love you deserve is revealed.

Drop
Negative Love Scripts
& Take Your Sacred Place

Society, upbringing, & love fog hand us countless negative love scripts to act out as if we had no other choice.

Consider the stories and myths in our culture which play out the desperate search for love. These stories are scripted with deep unfulfilled longings. We can easily find ourselves acting out these scripts of unrequited love – always searching and never fulfilling the search.

These negative love scripts are full of painful *"what ifs"* - part of the love fog which includes a huge clock that ticks away the seconds before your time runs outs to ever find love. The inner script sounds like this:

- *What if there isn't a love mate of my dreams?*
- *What if I can't find him or her?*
- *What if I am not qualified to be loved?*
- *What if my love mate is already taken?*
- *What if I am not good enough?*
- *What if my mate doesn't like the way I look?*
- *What if I am too old or not smart or rich enough?*

Listening to such spiritually unfounded but prevalent fears leads to love panic, hopelessness, and a willingness to settle for less than the love you deserve.

With Love's full support, you can choose to turn down all these negative love scripts. They cannot hold you in love bondage.

Who you are
is who you decide to be

No matter what negative love scripts you have previously accepted, they are no longer acceptable. Treat them as external and foreign to you and refuse to act them out. You have Love's authority for taking this stand.

Living beyond negative scripts, you are empowered to be who you really are in your heart, already claimed by Love and not needing to act as if you are not Love's own.

Think of the wonderful possibilities of Love beyond the fog. Love is, in this very moment, unfolding your life with the most original, individual, and beautiful Love plan, full of love-giving and love-receiving meant precisely and only for you.

Our hearts rejoice in advance for you as you proceed to take your sacred place as one peacefully preparing to meet your love mate, your love opport unities, and the love community that awaits you.

Be "In Love"
Now

Be in love right now.

This is the most natural state of your true being because your primary love relationship is – and always will be – with Love Itself.

Love
is calling you
to higher wisdom & bliss

We tend to think that being "in love" depends on the presence of another person and only then is love real and tangible. In truth, however:

Meeting a love mate is the outcome of Love, not the origin of love

All relationships spring forth from the one divine Source of Love. Rather than searching for love in thousands of places and moments, look out from Love and know that you are already there.

Take a moment and reflect: "How good is my present relationship with Love?"

Feel the presence of Love with you right now. Allow yourself to rest in this Love moment. Let Love speak to your heart. Listen to Love's message for you. Hear Love tell you of your vast importance to Love and your immense worth. Love cannot replace you. Love has a beautiful, fulfilling plan for your life. Love is telling you how precious you are and guiding you to know this.

Stay in this moment. Breathe in all the love you want. There is more waiting for you. Breathe in Love again. Permit Love to sink deep within your being and to let it dawn in your heart that you are truly not alone. Surrender to Love's caring for you. Accept Love as your constant companion. You are with Love. Love is with you. Love is in you. You and Love are *one*. You are in Love.

Let yourself fall in love with Love

This is the sacred place where all the love you deserve fuses as one giant light of Love. This is your true Love experience. This is the spiritual power Source which will generate all your love relationships forever. This is how you can connect with Love all the time. Getting here needs only the awakening and gentle opening of your heart.

You may say, *"I feel so alone."* In truth, none of us are alone because it is not possible for Love to be alone – or for you to be separated from Love.

Love's all-present Self is right now blessing, praising, adoring, understanding, calming, nurturing, and loving you. Love has never been absent from you. Love is always present with you. You are in Love's healing presence.

There is a painting of creation by Michelangelo in the Sistine chapel where God and man are reaching out to touch each other's hands. They come so close to touching but are short of contact by just a few inches. So close yet so far.

Our love pain comes from believing that we are so close to Love yet still so separate. We make the assumption that Love is not available, not present, not possible. The inches that divide us may as well be the distance covering the oceans.

Yet Infinite Love is present here, now, and always. There is no ocean to separate you from Love. Whenever you feel separated or distanced from Love, remind yourself that you are, in fact, united with Love. Love is present with you always. Feel Love's living presence with you now.

This is the reality that dissolves love fog with Love illumination. Knowing and claiming your oneness – your unity – with Love opens your life to Love's blessings for you. Each of us exists as Love's Presence – Love's Self. That is why we truly do meet and fall in love in Love's Light. Affirm to yourself:

> *My highest relationship – for eternity*
> *is with Love Itself &*
> *I am complete in Love right now*

Meet Your Love Mate In The Light

Love's lovers meet and unite in the Light.

The Light is who you truly are. The Light is also who your love mate truly is. The fusing of your Light with another's Light is what creates eternal Love.

That's why it is so important to release your love life to Love. Release your own predetermined outlining of what your love mate will look like, the way you will meet, or when this will happen.

Actively trust Love. Let Love surprise you. We wouldn't ever want to limit Love. Trusting love means opening your life to the infinite possibilities of Love waiting for you.

This is the hardest thing for lovers-in-waiting to do and we have great compassion for everyone desiring a love mate. Love, however, already has far more love in store for you than you could ever dream up or create yourself. Quite simply, Love is going to do a better job of bringing you to your love mate than you can do.

Let Love be the producer of your Love story

Here is a peek at what is going on behind the curtains as you let Love produce your love life. To begin with, Love sees your true beauty as the deep substance – the Light – within you. Think of what your Light looks like. Love already knows whose Light will most divinely fit with your Light. Isn't that beautiful? And it's true!

That's why it is so important to step into your Light. True lovers first meet in the Light of Love, not in a physical place – so turn up your radiance. Don't hide your spiritual identity. Discover who you are. Let your magnificence out of hiding. Be all of who you are. How can your love mate see you if your light is dim or invisible? Radiate love!

Let go of outlining how your love life is supposed to unfold. Love's plans for you are so much bigger! Let Love orchestrate. Let the brilliance of your love shine so brightly that your Light, *as* Love, creates the place, time, and circumstances that bring you and your love mate into spiritual synchronicity.

Open your consciousness to Love surprise! Let Love arrive in your life like a soft wind that appears out of nowhere when you open your divine senses to feel Love's breeze.

We both learned this great truth the hard way. In our first marriages, we met our partners in love fog rather than Light. We married for *form* more than *substance* and, as the marriages played out, what was obviously missing was the substance of genuine love.

After our marriages ended, we started asking ourselves, independently: *"What is it I am really looking for?"* And we both realized: *"I'm looking for the substance of love – for kindness, compassion, deep caring, listening, hearts connecting, joy, generosity, equality, harmony, spirituality, and for someone who has the capacity to love me as much as I can love."*

This is where your struggle ends and your new life of love begins. We had to come out of the love fog that led to so much suffering. We had to define love at a much higher level and rise to that higher level. In short, we had to dramatically revise our love standards to those in this book. We shifted our dreams to the Light and you are holding in this book the wonderful result of our taking this step. Please note that we took this leap *before* we met each other.

Take the leap into Light
before you meet
your beloved

We rejoice today in feeling like the happiest couple in the universe, but that seemed a preposterous, completely unreachable possibility before we made the shift to the higher love we both deserved.

We want you to have this experience of the love you deserve too. If today you are single, separated, or divorced and without a love mate, consider yourself *blessed* and *fortunate* rather than forsaken – because you have an advanced opportunity right now to get love right!

Practice
Loving

If you were an astronaut, you would practice repeatedly before you were sent into space – and you would not be sent until you were ready. Would you fly in a plane with a pilot that was not trained, or use a lawyer that had not studied law?

Yet how many of us have studied, practiced, and proved how to succeed in love! Is it any wonder that we struggle or fail?

*Envision this book as
an advanced training program
designed to enable you to become
an expert in love –
a LoveMaster*

Your practice of the 10 keys in this book will do even more than make you a great love mate. Your life will be so enhanced by your advanced love practice that potential love mates seeking genuine love will be attracted to you. Please expect this.

As you refine and polish your love skills, your love Light will become a beacon attracting your love mate and all those waiting to associate with you in Love. They will recognize you through Love's law of attraction. And just as importantly, *you* will recognize them.

Here's how you can practice loving. You may want to set these as Love goals and track your success. Be sure to praise yourself as you succeed.

- **Love yourself – deeply**. Take time to meditate and establish your clear intention to be at one with Love. Open your heart to loving your beautiful self as Love's creation. Your love mate from Love is already cherishing you this way. Love is loving you this way. Love your awakening Highest Self.

- **Be the presence of Love** everywhere you look, talk, walk, and think. Be a LoveMaster. All humanity needs your love and waits for it. Walk through life as the presence of Love, leaving a wake of goodwill, smiles, warmed hearts, and healing. Love humanity like you are going to love your love mate.

- **Develop a radiant, all-inclusive, healing Love practice**. Think of the millions of people who desperately need to feel loved. You can love these people right now. Recognize that Love heals. See yourself as Love's healing presence to those in need who you encounter – and those you cannot even see.

- **Be the love that you want to receive**. It is ironic that so many people who want to be treated with kindness, gentleness, and overflowing love do not treat others with these same qualities. Be wide awake to *being* the love you want to receive and become an expert with the love skills your love mate is eventually going to receive.

- **Love your future love mate right now**. Somewhere, right now, your future love mate is being prepared for you. You, too, are being prepared. Ask yourself: How well am I loving? Am I practicing the ten keys? Challenge yourself to become an expert at loving your future love mate right now. At this very moment, your love mate needs your love and will be vastly comforted by your loving thoughts and prayers for his or her wellness, encouragement, peace, progress, enlightenment, protection, and prosperity. Send compassion and healing and enjoy giving from your heart in this way. Your advanced cherishing will set a high spiritual tone when the relationship begins. We often remember how much we loved each other *before* we ever met.

- **Speak Love daily**. Say loving words. Address others as Love's own Presence. Tell them what you see as Love. Show them how precious they are. And see how precious you are as Love's presence to others. Speak Love heaven to them. Feel the joy of being at one with Love.

- **Build a Love community**. There is enormous support in practicing love relationships with others who are also on a spiritual path. Take courses, read books, and join with others who have common spiritual goals. See them as Love and practice acting from your Highest Self as Love. Everything you want in life can be experienced through the act of loving as Love.

- **Keep a Love journal**. Write down all the ways you loved others today and all the ways you were loved. Record your love goals for tomorrow. You will become powerfully conscious of living in Love reality rather than in love fog.

Loving well right now
is the most advanced opportunity
you have to move towards
the love you deserve

Flow With
Love Affirmations

Practice flowing with powerful Love affirmations that unite you with Love and attract all love to you. Write these on cards and place them around you as reminders to retrain your thought patterns.

We often use index cards for our affirmations – one for the desk and one for the bathroom mirror or pocket. The words are not powerful in themselves to manifest the love mate of your dreams. You need to embody these as your own thinking. For example, affirm:

- My Love prayers are already answered. At this very moment, Love is cherishing me and simultaneously cherishing my love mate.

- We are both being prepared to meet in the highest place of Love and nothing can prevent our meeting and recognizing each other.

- My love mate is already waiting for me. He or she will find me and nothing can separate us. Love will direct our meeting.

- Love is also steering me away from being mistakenly attracted to the wrong person.

- My love mate has the capacity to love me with all of Love's fullness.

- My love mate is already committed to esteem, support, adore, appreciate, praise, admire, enjoy, and nurture me. And I am joyfully committed to do this too.

- Love sees to it that we are divinely attracted, just as Love saw to it years ago that I would be divinely attracted to other wonderful things in my life.

- Love has been with me all along, knowing my needs in advance, caring for me, and preparing a path.

I am awake & open
to divine Love's blessings for me
& I am ready to be a blessing
to my love mate

Rise In Love
When You Meet
"The One"

Now comes the beautiful moment to put all your wonderful new love skills into play. You meet "The One!"

This is the exact moment to "rise in Love" rather than "fall in love."

It is so easy for our love meter to quickly go off the scale and register "This is the one!" without listening deeply for Love's guidance. False hope and self-deception can swiftly move us off Love's course.

If this is indeed the perfect love mate for you – direct from Love – Love will never let this relationship fail or slip away. So take this new opportunity to move gently forward in the Light.

Let this new relationship be a true Love meeting as you *begin* by establishing the most wonderful friendship. This is a perfect moment to reread the chapter on *Friendship First*. If this is true love, you are going to be friends for eternity. Your entire love success, in fact, will be built on the foundation of your friendship. So don't play games. Don't go into fantasy or romance consciousness. Stay in Love awakening and thoroughly relish your friendship.

If true love seems to be unfolding, read and discuss this book together. You will be amazed at how quickly you get to know a potential love mate through discussing this book. It will enhance your love and take you both to new heights.

Don't be afraid that taking this step might cause you to lose your potential love mate. Do you really want to keep a love mate who has no interest in genuine love?

For example, suppose your potential love mate responds to this idea with one of the following statements:

"I'm not interested in books on love."

"These books are all the same. They are only trying to force me to change from who I am."

"I'd love to discuss this book together. I want to love you well and I want to be well-loved."

Which of these love prospects is still in your life? If you can't discuss a book on genuine love with a potential love mate, how likely are you to ever experience genuine love with that person?

As your friendship expands to love, stay alert to your new relationship including all ten keys. So often the most loving people get picked by people who want love but have not done their own spiritual work. This causes a lopsided relationship of a giver and taker – or a giver and a less giver. You deserve a love mate with the same capacity to love you as you have – someone who registers high on Love's meter of genuine love giving.

If your love is not reciprocated equally, for example, this is certainly not the love mate you deserve. Question the continuing desire to hook up with someone that does not reciprocate your love in the fullest spirit of love.

Ask yourself, *"Am I telling myself that I am in love because I need a break from the fear that it might never happen?"*

What is Love telling you at your deepest level of intuition? You know!

Remember, you are not desperate. Love is never desperate. See the infinite nature of Love unfolding in your life. Every Love blessing is flowing to you with all the love you could ever want. Embrace it.

If you find that Love has indeed brought you two together, begin cherishing your relationship at the highest spiritual place. Feel the immense spiritual presence and support of both of you being on a spiritual path – already partners in spiritual growth.

Love
is right now
guiding you into Love completeness
& fulfillment in
the Light

Chapter 13

Expanding
A Relationship To
Ultimate Love

If you and your love mate are *eager* to expand your love – or simply *willing* to expand your love – that says a lot of good about the quality of your love.

To be open to more love shows an understanding that Love's possibilities for you and your partner are infinite. Here are some excellent ways to open your relationship to the infinite possibilities of Love:

Read this Book
Together

Sharing feelings is often easier for women.

Several of the men on our review team privately acknowledged how difficult it is for them to share their feelings. It's not that they are unreceptive to sharing. They are simply inexperienced in sharing.

Yet these men are dedicated to expanding their relationships with their love mate. This is all the opening that genuine love needs.

Genuine love
is like brilliant light
that sneaks through the cracks
in our consciousness
when we open ourselves to growth
&
we can never return
to darkness

Set New Standards For Your Relationship

As you share your feelings with each other, use this book to set new standards for your relationship:

- Share your answers together *on The Love You Deserve* quiz.
- Go through each of *the 10 Keys to Genuine Love* and openly discuss your feelings, needs, and desires.
- Identify what would move your love relationship to a 10 in each key.
- Identify how you can help each other grow.

Give Gratitude

Gratitude makes the heart sing. You cannot overdo gratitude. Make a list right now of the 5 ways that you most value your love mate:

1. _____
2. _____
3. _____
4. _____
5. _____

Does your love mate know about this list? Don't let it be a secret. Share it openly.

On our monthly wedding anniversaries (we count them by months because we are so happy together), we often share why we love each other – the little ways and big ways. It's an extraordinary and enlightening sharing and brings us even closer. It also reminds us of our enormous value to each other.

Identify Even More Ways of Being Intimate

Intimacy brings us to the heart of genuine love – and intimacy often means different things to each partner. Take a moment and list 5 things *you* could do to bring more intimacy to your relationship:

1. _____
2. _____
3. _____
4. _____
5. _____

What are 5 ways your partner could bring more intimacy to your relationship?

1. _____
2. _____
3. _____
4. _____
5. _____

Remember, this is not an exercise in what the other person is failing to do. It is an exercise of letting each of your hearts move higher in unity. The goal is more intimacy, not judgment. The goal is more love. So keep your hearts open and sweet. Find ways to laugh with each other and not be defensive. You may be treading on tender emotions, but keep reminding each other that you are in a wonderful process of elevating your relationship.

Practice
The Love You Deserve

Give yourself the advanced love assignment of practicing the love described in this book – living the 10 keys. When you take this step, you will be surprised and pleased how quickly your relationship will expand to new heights.

The 10 keys are not abstract or theoretical. They are practical, straight-forward, and easy to understand.

- Don't let pride, frustration, lack of patience, or "You go first" stop you from being a genuine lover.
- Rate yourself on your own expertise with the 10 keys and don't settle for less than a 9.
- Practice on your weak areas with the commitment to become a LoveMaster.
- Love yourself as you grow.

Only
the practice of loving
makes us
LoveMasters

Open Your Mind & Heart To Love As Infinite

Ultimate love is infinite – without boundaries, measurement, beginning, or end. Love is expanding forever without interruption – and you are in the center of this Love. This Love is what best identifies you and your love mate. This very Love Presence brought you together and is the love you two share.

To see Love from this spiritual perspective opens all the possibilities. How high can Love go? No limit!

If we think that we, ourselves, are manufacturing Love, this will have limits on how far we can expand, but spiritual Love has no limits. That's why it's so important to see your relationship spiritually.

Each of us face our relationship with a choice.

One, we can occasionally think of our love partners as spiritual or when we are in the right mood or setting.

Two, we can consistently see each other as spiritual – all the time and as a top priority. That means cherishing each other's highest spiritual identity daily through the eyes of Love. It means praying for each other as spiritual beings and flowing with affirmations of reverence for our spiritual identities and the fusion of our Light together.

Reverence for each other
as spiritual beings
is the gateway to
infinite love

From this spiritual place of infinite love possibilities, there are no boundaries to the love you two can share.

In our marriage, we often feel as if there are more than just the two of us. There is what we sometimes refer to as the "Presence of the Third" – Love Itself guiding, orchestrating, fulfilling, and celebrating our union.

Let the
Presence of the Third
grace your love

This is the inevitable result of a relationship based on spiritual Love. When two people see their relationship as spiritual, they live in Love space where they feel the overwhelming and infinite support of divine Love. This openness and commitment to spiritual Love creates the divine Love magic where two lovers expanding in spiritual Love experience "1 plus 1" equals infinity rather than "2."

This Presence of Love is the foundation of every spiritual relationship. After all, you came together because you saw the divine Self in each other. That's the Presence of Love in your lives and it is easy to forget when errands, kids, work, stress, conflict, and daily interruptions flow through your lives.

Constantly acknowledge the true substance of your love as spiritual. Remember, you are not seeking infinite Love outside yourself. Your relationship is flowing with infinite Love from *within*. This is Love's view of your relationship and the understanding that takes love mates into bliss and ecstasy.

Let your vision of the relationship
move into eternity and timeless being
where your union together
reconnects you with who you truly are – at
one with Love

Let Your Relationship Embrace The World

Let your expanding Love relationship embrace the world.

A relationship that is focused inward may seem joyous and complete, but to expand in infinite Love we need to open our hearts so wide that they include and embrace all humanity.

We've all seen people madly in love, completely oblivious to anything or anyone else. That's natural, of course, when someone is first in love. Yet those of us on the outside of that wonderful joy can easily feel excluded. That's why we need to stay tuned to Love as all-embracing. Infinite Love is the very opposite of excluding. Love, by it's nature, is all-inclusive.

This is one of the key secrets of our own love success. People often say to us, *"I feel so loved in your presence."* What they are actually experiencing is the universal, all-inclusive nature of our love that is so infinite that it could not possibly exclude anyone. And this universal embracing never detracts from the immensity of love we share with each other. Love is infinite.

A wonderful way of expanding your relationship in Love is to ask the transforming question,

What is the highest purpose
of our relationship?

What is our mission statement
as a couple?

There is no right or wrong answer to these questions, of course, because Love is infinite. But asking these questions instantly places you into infinite, expanding Love flow.

To think in terms of your relationship's value to the world brings spiritual illumination to why you have been brought together by Love.

See Yourself Advancing In Infinite Love

Love is always advancing because it is infinite and, as Love's own expression, you are part of that infinite advance. Love is never static. So Love's infinite advancing means there will be constant expansion – constant change – in your relationship.

Without spiritual perspective, however, we often resist change. We might feel, *"I'm happy just the way we are. I don't want anything to change" or "I haven't had time to adjust to the last Love change."*

Quite often, change feels like human stress. But going deeper, change is about making the higher decision to live more congruently with your divinity.

Think of infinite Love as continually refining your character and elevating your relationship. Love wants you to become even more loving. Love wants you to replace all judging with total honoring and to release ego for your divine Self. It is natural for you to expand in Love in these ways because you are part of Love's infinite flow and expansion.

Genuine love is like an infinite river
always flowing & carving
out new beauty & life

Chapter 14

Flowing With Love
In Hard Times

If we had read this book during our previous marriages, we would have been silently mourning, thinking to ourselves:

"I'll never experience such love. I'm immersed in a relationship with little hope of fulfillment, not to mention genuine love."

Today we are writing to you from the very heart of genuine love.

Were we failures because of our failed marriages? No! We had simply not awakened to genuine love as our spiritual right. Were either of our ex-spouses failures? No! None of us were awake to genuine love. There were loving moments, but the idea of our *spiritual right* to genuine love was not established.

Yet all that time, we were being prepared and loved by Love:

- This book could not have come forth nor speak to you with authenticity without our experiences of *failed* love.
- This book could also not have come forth without our experience of *genuine* love.

- We give deep gratitude for these experiences in love.
- We feel great compassion for those currently struggling for happiness with a love mate.
- We have learned and grown spiritually.
- We now understand, with the spiritual authority that comes from being at one with Love, that genuine love belongs to *each* of us.

Here are some ways to move to higher ground in your love life.

Choose To Go Higher
When Disagreements Come

Every relationship is going to be challenged with problems. The key to love is not to let challenges divide you from within.

A powerful defense is to look at problems as challenges to the relationship itself. See them as opportunities to demonstrate your mutual love and deepen the reasons that you united in the first place. It's all about growing together in love.

We are all learning lessons. Every challenge is a turning point – a choice. Will you allow yourself to fall into the trap of resentment and hold on to anger, blame, and hurt feelings? Or will you choose the high ground and practice loving each other well?

You may think, *"Easy for Scott and Shannon to say. They have such a loved-filled easy life."* The truth is that every solid love relationship gets tested – and tested frequently. Every couple experiencing genuine love has been through painful experiences that have forced them to grow higher in Love. So too with us, but we live by a very potent love strategy for dealing with disagreements:

When we disagree,
we don't go forward until
we have a solution that genuinely satisfies
both of us

Practicing this principle leads to wonderful and surprising love solutions. By practicing this love principle with even the smallest disagreements, you become more expert at moving to this high love space with more demanding challenges.

We remember a great moment of stress when there were many deadlines and many pressures. We were both about to explode. Instead, the depth of our commitment to genuine love led us to take each other's hands – in long silence. As we let the steam dissolve, we looked into each other's eyes. We re-connected with Love.

Taking such a critical moment to connect with Love is the difference between a relationship skidding downwards and a relationship moving higher in love. It takes courage, forgiveness, and true love to stay in the challenging moment with love, but if you don't, trying to repair the relationship an hour, day, or week later is going to be a lot tougher.

It's the same with name calling or belittling. We never go there. First, because it is so out of sync with everything we know about Love. And second, because such damage to a relationship is sometimes impossible to repair. Such actions bruise the heart. Is that what you really intend?

Another strain on a relationship comes from baggage we bring into the relationship. It might be our past relationships or a family member that is difficult. Such challenges can cause partners great division. But this again goes back to how we define what's happening. It's helpful to look at something like this as a challenge to the relationship itself because, really, if you get sucked into complaining about parents, kids, or relatives, you are going to create friction and disharmony within your relationship. It's really an opportunity not to judge, to practice being a more loving person, to see from another person's point of view, and to support your love mate.

For example, one partner has already carried the burden of the relationship with the child, past relationship, or relative for a long time alone. The partner who has not carried the burden can come in with a fresh new sense of compassion and help lift the load by adding empathy and understanding and be a new voice of healing influence in these situations.

Call
"The Love Truck"
Immediately

If your house was on fire, you might first try a fire extinguisher, but if the fire was too big, you'd call the fire department – immediately!

Now, if the fire department was 10 miles away, your whole house might burn down before the fire trucks arrived.

When a couple has a conflict or disagreement, there is plenty of heat that can spark a fire in the relationship. The critical love questions are:

- Will you, or won't you, call the Love truck?
- How long will it take the Love truck to arrive?

The longer it takes for the Love truck to arrive, the more likely you are to have a deteriorating, destroyed, or smoldering relationship.

In our marriage, we think of the Love truck as being parked in our garage. When we have a disagreement, we call for the Love truck within minutes, usually seconds – and it arrives instantly.

And what does the Love truck bring? Instead of water to put out the fire, it pours out forgiveness and patience and sweetness and then humor and goodwill and apologies and kindness and softness.

Become an expert at getting the Love truck to your love challenges instantly. The benefits are extraordinary. Not only will the specific fire – disagreement – get put out, but you will find yourself soon laughing and loving each other again rather than living in smoking silence or potential ruins.

It takes love wisdom to park the Love truck in your garage. And it takes love courage to call it instantly, but this is what flowing with love in hard times is all about.

As soon as
there is a dispute or argument,
get the "Love Truck"
rolling

Use The
Powerful Healing Strategy
"Let's Pray"

Here's another approach we use to solve problems. When we have a disagreement that is getting intense and we can't seem to find mutual love ground, we often say:

Let's pray about this
and get Love's highest answer

That takes the problem to a whole new dimension of healing where a wonderful solution can come forward without the pressure of time or personal persuasion. We put the disagreement on hold until Love speaks.

This gives much-needed breathing room and serves as a turning to divine Love for the higher answer. We do this constantly, and by the next day or hour, the most original solutions come forth – that both of us love.

This divine pause for a higher answer gives each partner time to silently reconsider and listen to the other partner's position and reasoning. Humorously enough, we often switch sides after such spiritual Love reflection.

Going to Love for the higher solution awakens both partners from the dream of division because, at the highest spiritual level, there are not two minds. There is only one Mind – the mind of infinite Love. As we align ourselves with this infinite Mind of all-intelligent, all knowing love and harmony, we wake up from division and see our lives from a place of great spiritual harmony. It's a beautiful way of healing and flowing with love in hard times.

Move Forward at Love Speed

Often in a relationship, one partner is ready to go "forward" faster than another. One partner may be raring to go while the other is still pondering or unsure.

This is a perfect time to listen to Love and allow the right solution to come forward at Love speed. In our marriage, we practice this principle of moving forward at Love speed – and Love speed is rather hard to nail down. Sometimes, Love causes us to move very, very slowly. At other times, Love moves us so fast that transformation takes place instantly.

Let yourself flow at Love's speed

Love speed sometimes feels like going at the pace of the slowest partner, but something much deeper is actually taking place. Both partners commit to placing the issue in Love's hands and listening honestly to Love's direction.

We find, in our marriage, that we have frequent role reversals here. Sometimes Scott is the fast one. Sometimes Shannon. We have lots of opportunities to practice moving at Love speed.

Forgive Quickly

"Shannon, something I admire in you so much that you really taught me is to forgive quickly. Really, you forgive instantly."

"Thank you Scott. I can't stand not to forgive. Grudges just don't make sense. It's always a choice – for all of us."

In our marriage, we have a silent agreement that when one of us apologizes, the other moves into acceptance as quickly as possible – and most of the time, it is immediate. This is very healing.

Learn to forgive quickly. This is really what love is all about. Get the big picture. If you could look back on your relationship from the future, you would instantly see how unproductive it was not to forgive.

During the time you don't forgive, your love will be deteriorating, not getting stronger. Forgiving doesn't mean you are weak. It takes love strength to forgive. The person who forgives is taking the leadership in creating the opportunity for a relationship to flow with love in hard times. If, however, you are faced with forgiving abuse, there are a different set of rules. Please see the chapter *Healing Hurt & Abuse.*

Set the Stage For
Love Progress

Growth is often invisible and easy to overlook.

Just think how much struggle and growth is taking place within your private consciousness right now – that only you know about. Much of what is stirring within you may seem hard, even impossible, to talk about with others or your love mate.

This same growth is taking place within *all* of us –
even within your love mate.

***Don't be fooled into thinking that
someone is not growing
simply because
you cannot see it***

Growth first takes place deep in our being – and
then in our actions. With this awareness, reach out
to your love mate with all the skills you have learned
in this book.

- Tell your love mate that you want to grow
  together positively, not negatively.
- Love your love mate the way you would like
  to be loved.
- Be open in discussing your needs and desires with your love mate. Don't be afraid.
  Love is expressing you. Ask for your love
  mate's support.
- Ask your love mate what he or she would
  most like from you to improve the relationship.
- Demonstrate listening, cherishing, and
  honoring of your love mate.
- See your love mate as spiritual. You may
  have entirely different views, but viewing and
  praising the beauty of your love mate's
  spiritual qualities will enable you to speak to
  the highest good within your love mate.

***Speak to the King or Queen
within your love mate
and you will see the
King or Queen
come forth***

Set Standards
for The Love You Deserve

Personal love standards set the mark for the highest place you want to live in Love. They also clarify what you are unwilling to accept in love.

Whether your love mate is responsive or not, set standards for the love *you* deserve.

If your love mate does not care about your love needs, the real issue is not your love mate's attitude but whether *you* are willing to accept a lower standard of love than you deserve.

With all that you have invested in your love relationship, it is natural to try to raise your relationship to your new awareness of genuine love rather than to simply walk away.

This is an opportunity not to condemn your love mate, but to lovingly explain a higher standard of love that can reward each of you – to explore the possibilities of *more* love in your lives together.

It is also an opportunity to love yourself enough to be honest with your love mate about your needs and desires.

If, after you have won a gold medal for your love skills of communicating to your love mate with honesty & kindness, your partner still expresses no interest in growing, you have to ask the tough questions:

- Is this really love?
- Am I willing to accept this lower standard of "love" for the rest of my life?
- Am I staying in the relationship because I feel pity for my love mate? Or fear of what might happen?

- Do I love myself enough to take a stand for genuine love?

"But I'll be all alone if I leave," you may fear. The truth is that if you stay in such a relationship, you may be even more alone. The long-term pain of staying in the relationship may be worse than the short-term pain of separation. Ask yourself, *"Where do I want to be a year from now – still stuck in this relationship because I wouldn't face being alone?"*

Of course, if children are involved, that may shift the entire equation.

Before you contemplate any stand, surround yourself with friends that love you, keep practicing your highest love skills with your love mate, and listen keenly to your spiritual intuition for Love's highest answer.

Don't Have An Affair

It is natural that during hard times in a love relationship, you might be tempted to seek love with another person who seems more loving. However, having an affair while you are in a committed relationship:

- Does not solve your love problems. It worsens them. It prevents you from moving forward effectively with either relationship.
- Avoids the real issue of facing up to your love mate and taking steps towards healing – whether that means working to improve your relationship or separating.
- Violates the very fabric of genuine love because you would be acting outside honesty, kindness, and spirituality.

- Confuses and abuses being true to your own emotions and to your integrity.

Love yourself enough
to bring your present relationship
to healing or closure

There *Is* A Healing Solution

Solutions come to us in unexpected ways.

Do you know the story of the man whose house was flooding? A neighbor in a boat came to rescue him but he declined the help, saying:

"God will save me!"

The flood waters rose and soon the man had to climb to his second floor to stay above the water line. Another rescue boat arrived. He shouted:

"No thanks. God will save me!"

But the waters kept rising. Standing on his roof with flood waters almost washing his house away, a helicopter let down its rescue ladder. But the man wouldn't take it. He soon drowned in the waters.

Arriving in heaven, he asked:

"Why, God, would you not save me?"

And God replied:

"Well, I sent two boats and a helicopter!"

We need to be alert to solutions. If we don't expect one, or if we have pre-determined what the solution must be, we are unlikely to see it when it arrives.

Unlike the man in the flood who had little understanding of God, look out from a mental position that acknowledges God as infinite Love and feel Love embracing your entire life.

- You are not trapped.
- This is your opportunity to grow.
- Expect to be loved.
- Don't refuse Love's solutions.
- Listen to Love for comfort, encouragement, & guidance
- Let Love open the way for you.
- Be alert to *Love's* solutions!

**When
we acknowledge
the power & presence of Love
we open ourselves to
Love's healing solutions**

Take A Stand
For Healing

If a relationship is in hard times because of misfortune in business, job, career, finance, or heath, the answer may be to unite together in even higher love and use the storm as an opportunity to strengthen your love.

If, however, a relationship is truly in hard times where one partner is angry or mean to the other, or both are angry, this condition is not a solution. Something has to change.

Unfortunately, in many relationships facing hard times, things don't change and these partners live in perpetual misery.

It takes courage to take a stand for healing, but that is the only step that will put your lives back into love. Remember, you entered the relationship for love, not pain.

At some point we have to love ourselves enough to draw a line in the sand and say, "That's it, crossing here means there will be consequences."

Here's what such love leadership might look like in a conversation with your partner. You might say:

"We are both obviously struggling and unhappy in our relationship. Rather than trying to figure out who's at fault, let's take our relationship to a healing place so we can both experience more love. If we don't, our relationship will most likely deteriorate and end. I want you to know that I'm here in the space of receptivity to healing and loving each other forward. I hope that you will enter that same space with me."

Who could resist such an invitation?

Well, the sad truth is that many partners do resist that invitation. It's a resistance to Love itself. But this is where not accepting the status quo becomes so powerful. The person who creates the opening for the relationship by saying, "Let's go forward with healing" is on strong Love ground.

If the other person doesn't want to flow with more love, then that really is a crucial turning point for the relationship. It is one more step that says, "Hmm, maybe this relationship isn't right." That won't make you happy, but it puts the relationship into love honesty.

Trust
Your Intuition

A spiritual mentor, an expert on healing, once shared a valuable truth: *"Never give advice."*

As much as any of us may think we know what is right for another person, it is not our place in the universe to tell another person what decision to make in a relationship. The highest position of loving another person is to affirm that divine Love is guiding and supporting that person – and to provide all the listening, cherishing, and honoring we know how to give.

And, even more importantly, listen to your own intuition. As you listen quietly and unreservedly to Love, you will hear Love's truth speaking directly to you, guiding you intelligently with comfort and with Love's honest and highest solution.

The highest position
you can take in loving yourself
is to trust your own spiritual intuition

Be The One
To Execute The Vision

When you listen honestly to your own intuition – your deepest spiritual insight – Love's heart will always give you the highest answer. Unfortunately, we often seek the approval of others before we act on our own spiritual vision. But our true spiritual power comes from trusting Love's direct voice to our inner, highest self, our intuition. As Shannon so often states:

The person with the vision
has to execute
the vision

We have openly shared our vision of genuine love in this book – and we've done so without asking if others approve. We have shared the song in our hearts – direct from our personal experience and spiritual intuition – as a gift to you.

You, too, must sing your song. Your love mate does not control your song. When struggling for happiness in a relationship, we may be tempted to want our love mate to be the one to change, but the higher, more powerful approach is to dig into our own intuition for our vision of what we want and need and then execute this vision ourselves.

Here's an example from Scott's life – in his own words:

After six years in a previous marriage that had good moments, but was unhappy for both of us, I wrestled my way towards a clear vision. After years of hoping that the love I thought I was expressing would result in a transformed marriage, I realized my mistake. I was waiting for my wife to change rather than taking a stand for what I knew in my intuition was right for me. I remember walking down the hall in our home and saying to her, with kindness but honesty:

> *"We need to commit to either improving our marriage or else end it. Do you want to work on it?"*

To my surprise, she said *"No."* But the honesty of this moment and my willingness to execute the vision I knew was right led to an amicable divorce. I had taken a step towards the love I deserved. And, in her truthfulness, so had she.

Know that during every moment you struggle for happiness in a relationship, you are not alone. Your friends are with you. We are with you. Thousands of people are supporting you with love that you cannot see. Most importantly:

Love Itself
Is cherishing you and leading you
to the love you deserve

Chapter 15

Healing
Hurt & Abuse

Nothing is so disempowering as hurt and abuse. This is a subject that easily evokes tears, but we write this chapter to you expecting a great deal of healing.

We want you to know that no matter how much hurt or abuse you have experienced, we cherish you, honor you, and deeply believe that your heart can heal.

Let's begin by being very alert to what abuse is.

Physical abuse is obvious – throwing objects at a partner, hitting, or harming. The statistics on this are terrible. About every 9 seconds in the United States, another woman is physically abused. Statistics show that about 22% of women have been physically abused at one point in their life and 8% of men. And if it weren't for shame, there would perhaps be far more people who would admit to being victims. Physical abuse is intolerable and totally unacceptable.

Emotional abuse is less obvious – name calling, condemning, and demeaning – but equally abusive. It's less obvious because, on the same day you've been called a name, your partner may also tell you how much he or she loves you. Or beg for your forgiveness. That's confusing. So we tend to tolerate it, live with it, and get used to it. That is how uncertain we are about loving ourselves and knowing that we deserve to be loved with honoring and *zero* abuse.

Another type of abuse we carry within us is the collection of our own past failures, hurts, and rejections. Past hurts need to be cleansed and healed from our lives.

Many people live their lives almost exclusively in the past, even though they are free to step into the freedom of Love space right now.

Those raised without love or approval, for example, may suffer from the abuse of trying hard for acceptance and love. They may set themselves up for being controlled according to whether people surrounding them approve of them or not.

Please know that you are not damaged and that you can rise into Love's completely loving and healing place for your life.

Living totally without abuse is your spiritual right. In fact, it is your spiritual right to experience the exact opposite of abuse.

The opposite of abuse is honoring & deep cherishing of who you are

That is the love you deserve!

Here are some empowering principles for healing hurt and abuse in your life.

See Yourself As Completely Worthy of All Love

You are so worthy of all love. Our hearts beg you to love yourself – and we support you in advance.

What is the inner voice saying to resist this wonderful idea of more genuine love for you? Maybe your parents or someone else told you that you were unworthy or unimportant.

Believing these negative thoughts about yourself is a roadblock to your experience of the love you deserve. The moment has come to release all negativity about yourself no matter who said it or how many times it was said, or for how long. How much longer will you allow the cruelty of someone else's poor treatment and judgment of you determine your present state of happiness?

When will the moment be more appropriate than now for you to reject whatever toxic things have been said about you or to you? It is time to step outside the old self and move past the sludge of other people's negative judgments.

Step into your Highest Self and flow with self-honoring, self-comfort, & highest valuing of yourself

It is not egotistical to love yourself. Be very clear about that. It is Love's intention that all of us are deeply loved.

Begin releasing negative thoughts about your worth and replace them with higher thoughts of who you truly are. For example, here are some negative thoughts you may be rehearsing and need to replace:

- "I'm not worthy of love."
- "I don't think highly of myself because I feel guilty about the past."
- "I've been a failure all my life at getting people to love me."
- "I will never succeed in love because there is too much wrong with me."
- "I will never get past my hurt or abuse."

Now let's do a healing exchange to take your life into Love's wisdom. Affirm to yourself these higher truths about yourself:

- I *am* worthy of all love because I am from the divine source of Love which embraces me in pure Love.
- I naturally include success in love and a life free from guilt because this is my divine heritage.
- If there are things I need to forgive myself for, I can do this now because I have more than enough love to cover my wrongs and bring me back into the Light. I feel clean and good about myself – regardless of what anyone else thinks about me.
- I choose these higher thoughts and I realize that this is only the beginning of viewing myself through the eyes of Love.
- I agree to have more gentleness, tenderness, and compassion for myself.
- I can learn from wisdom how to trust in Love.
- I know Love loves me this way and I accept this blessing now.

Set A
New Love Standard
For Yourself

Let this book be a full description of *your* new love standards.

One woman who had been raised in an abusive environment wrote to us:

> *"I had almost given up hope that the love described in this book was possible. The 10 keys so beautifully articulated are my new measuring stick for all future love mates. I'm no longer willing to compromise."*

Today, this woman has become a LoveMaster – an expert in loving others, but also an expert in loving herself. She now lives in the consciousness and freedom of knowing that it is her spiritual right to be well loved. She offers herself love in new, caring ways each day. She has fallen in love with Love – and with herself as Love's beautiful being. You can do this too.

You are 100% worthy
of being genuinely & completely
loved at the highest level
of Love Itself

Ground Your Identity in Healing Prayer

The most important thing you can do in every circumstance of hurt is to pray. Listen to Love's wisdom to guide you to love-centered people and away from those who speak and act in ways that hurt your feelings.

You don't have to stay with these people to make things right. Remove yourself and be guided in Love's higher plan for your life.

Through prayer you can lean on divine Love to comfort you and lift you to higher ground. In divine Love, there is no record of hurt, only a record of your preciousness. Love never lapses from Her sweet nature and condition and, in Truth, neither have you. And Love never abuses. Love honors.

***Let yourself feel the infinite honoring
of divine Love cherishing you
to your core***

Forgive Others & Forgive Yourself

Forgiveness is a powerful act of moving away from hurt and abuse and towards loving yourself.

Without forgiveness, our lives continue to spiral downwards, coiled in the web of the past.

Ask yourself, what would my life be like if I forgave those who have hurt me? Imagine your new personal freedom. The alternative is to experience even more years holding on to hurt – all that lost opportunity to embrace Love and move into freedom. Is this really the life you want?

There are many excuses for not forgiving:

- They don't deserve to be forgiven.
- They might do it again if I forgive.
- They may think I agree with them if I forgive.
- I don't want to give up my anger.
- Holding on to the hurt is my defense from being hurt again.

This is not living the life you deserve. Holding on to anger is a decision to suffer. Let the transforming light of Love flow into your heart and release the pain that has attached itself to you. Allow Love to bring fresh, healing renewal to your heart.

Even though you may never go back to a relationship, it needs forgiveness – because *you* deserve forgiveness. Lack of forgiveness interferes with your ability to feel truly loved. When you let go of negative feelings, you let the hole in your heart heal through the power of forgiveness.

It is important to understand that forgiveness does not mean that abusive behavior may continue. Forgiveness means something changes in the relationship permanently. It means that you have made the decision to move away from the hurt and abuse. It means you have chosen to empower yourself and act on your decision for better love.

Ask yourself,

"What would it take for me to let go and forgive?

Do I really serve myself or the world by hanging on to bad feelings about myself or others?"

Throw Out Your Container of Past Hurt

Just as you clean your home, you need to regularly clean out negative thinking to make room for grander concepts of Love.

Rather than being a container for suffering and hurt and an endless rehearsal of pain, be a container for Light, inspiration, and Love.

Suppose you had your entire collection of memories of hurt and abuse stored in a big heavy trunk in your home. Now suppose you could have the entire trunk permanently removed from your mental home. That's how you can think of any unhealed hurts and fears. Stop being a storage container for them. Release them to Love.

When we married, Scott was still holding on to some past hurt. Shannon encouraged him to dump the past and refuse to be a container for such thinking. This support was enormously liberating.

You too can be a container for uplifting, empowering thoughts about yourself, your divine origin, and all the new ideas you are learning from Love in this book. Listen for divine guidance and let Love tell you what belongs in your thinking.

***Mentally argue
on the side of good
as though you were a top-notch lawyer
hired to defend your happiness***

This is what it means to love yourself and what it looks like to have the love you deserve.

Have A Relationship
With Love, Not
Hurt

What do you have a relationship with when you carry around negative feelings of hurt, resentment, and rejection? You have a relationship with hurt, resentment, and rejection. The actual relationship you had in the past has been transformed into a new *present* relationship – a relationship not with a person but with hurt itself.

In our marriage, whenever one of us says something such as, *"I'm still struggling with what someone said or the way I was treated,"* we go into instant healing mode. *"Wait a minute,"* we realize, *"this is a relationship I am having with the hurt, not the person, and I don't need to continue a relationship with hurt."*

This awareness brings an immediate decision to stop rehearsing or holding on to the relationship with hurt.

It is your
constant opportunity
to have a relationship exclusively
with Love, not with hurt

Let Love redefine your past. So often we allow ourselves to be judged by what occurred in our past. Yet we grow and develop and we really do change and improve, especially if we are on a spiritual path. The major changes we make in our lives as a result of spiritual growth should be credited in our own view of ourselves today. We deserve the credit.

Here is an exercise to help redefine yourself as separate from any former negative feelings associated with your love life. Please pause. Take in the big picture of your love life and ask, *"What have I learned?"*

This question creates an enormous consciousness shift away from failure thinking. The only question that matters concerning your love history is this: *"What have I learned?"*

This question redefines your love history from a time of "hurt or failure" to a time of "great learning." Your spiritual growth is the real history.

Appreciate that you are on a learning curve. This Earth experience is a school of lessons. The sooner we get the lessons learned, the sooner we check them off our list and graduate to higher Love learning. We are all learning.

"Learning" cancels "failing"
and takes your love experience to a
spiritual place
of acquiring true Love wisdom

We both had failed earlier marriages and it is almost embarrassing to think of what we didn't know. Yet we learned such valuable lessons that today we are experiencing the deepest love we ever imagined.

That's why it is so valuable to redefine your personal history. Even in talking about our past relationships, we have helped each other recognize that the mistakes we made were for learning. So honor yourself and step away from rehearsing regret which is really self-abuse.

Here is an example of what Shannon learned looking back on the time that her ex-husband left her. In her words:

"I listened for divine guidance after my separation from my ex-husband. The spiritual work I did during those early months actually led me to greater love.

Although I had experienced emotional hurt after he left, it actually turned into a magnificent lesson and blessing. I learned that I deserved to be far more equally loved and cherished.

Then I met Scott. That wouldn't have happened if I hadn't been left by my ex-husband. Rejection is not the worst thing that can occur. It is often the result of the spiritual guidance we pray for.

In fact, during Scott's and my courtship, I was still struggling with the feelings of hurt and rejection from my previous marriage. But Scott was rejoicing – and reminded me that he and I would otherwise not be together. Looking back, I can see with perspective. That's why I often ask myself when I experience a change, 'How is eternity recording this?'"

Get the big picture of your real history – the spiritual viewpoint. We are here to learn lessons and grow spiritually. No one can achieve that goal without mistakes. Love yourself as you grow. The lessons of wisdom are hard to learn, and when we learn them, we must remain alert so we won't repeat them.

Let your history show that you are walking forward after surviving many storms, obstacles, and defeats. You are a success. You survived. You have learned so much. Make a short list of what you have learned from past relationships:

- _____
- _____
- _____
- _____
- _____

**Love yourself
forward**

Take A Love Stand
For Healing or An Ending

What if your relationship is stuck in abuse and your partner is trying to convince you that *you* are wrong and that you deserve to be ashamed and hurt?

Condemnation and shaming are very powerful weapons of sustained abuse – but they cannot stand against genuine Love.

This is where you take your Love stand. Do you want to stay connected to someone so dis-empowering?

In your Love stand, communicate clearly that your present relationship is not working for you.

***No matter how long
you have tolerated abuse in the past,
it is no longer acceptable***

Explain firmly and lovingly that you refuse to live your life from such an un-empowering place and without true honoring.

It is easier to say these words, of course, than to put them into action. In many abusive relationships, the person being abused feels powerless to change.

Don't allow intimidation or fear tactics to cower you from speaking up for the love you deserve.

You are not stuck. Your love life is not hopeless, although it may be with this particular person unless there is a significant shift higher. Remember, Love is with you right this moment.

In all honesty, there are three choices for your relationship.

One, the status quo – living in abuse for the rest of your life. Two, healing – where the relationship dramatically improves and you begin to experience the love you deserve. Or three, the end of the relationship where you have the courage to bring to an end a relationship that simply won't budge from abuse.

Since the status quo is unacceptable, decide in your own mind that the only options left in your relationship are either healing or an ending. Now you can speak with love and authority. You might say to your partner – with kindness, love, and honesty:

"I'm not happy with our relationship and I'm unwilling to accept the status quo – things as they are – any more. I hope we can have open conversations to see if we can become happier and more comfortable in sharing our love and moving away from hurt for me.

I am committed to working on healing our relationship if you are. We've come to the place where our relationship either moves higher in healing or it comes to an end so that I won't have to live in any more abuse. This is what I need to do out of love for myself and out of love for you us well."

Do you see the no nonsense attitude about this? This is the attitude you will need to adopt in order to turn things around from abuse to self-respect.

Condemnation and blame are big tools for people who practice abuse to others. You don't need to understand why they do it. Just decide that it is no longer acceptable and the guilt inflicted won't work on you ever again. Genuine love never imposes guilt.

We have seen many physical problems healed as a result of a person's decision to end the practice of being victimized, whether by name calling, blame, accusation, or domination.

*Great healing takes place
when we take a stand against abuse
& for
our self-respect*

Step Out of Abuse

As hard as taking this step may seem, it is your spiritual right to step out of abuse.

Abuse continues in our lives when abuse is:

- Not identified.
- Kept a secret.
- Left alone.
- Continues after being addressed.

Nothing is more enabling to abuse then excusing it and allowing it to continue. Often in Shannon's healing practice, she hears abused women excuse their lover's behavior either through sympathy for them or by explaining that they only do it occasionally. Then she hears these woman say how wonderful their partners are 85% of the time. This is an attitude of tolerance where zero tolerance should be.

If you are with someone who abuses you, let go of the idea that you must stay together. Do the loving thing for *your* life and step out of the relationship. Give yourself the opportunity to heal in an emotionally safe environment.

Don't return to the relationship unless your partner has genuinely and fully apologized and changed so dramatically that you are sure that he or she will never abuse you again.

And don't allow yourself to be brought back through cheap words of empty, insincere promises giving you false hope. Action and reform are all that count. Nothing short of this could possibly win you back.

So often we don't make a change because we think we will wind up alone. But you will never be alone when you stay in Love. Allow Love to re-create your life to higher, more loving place.

For Shannon, being alone after her ex-husband left gave her an opportunity to do important thinking about her life and decisions. She was able to think independently for herself and reason through what would make her happy and what standards she would set to avoid past mistakes. Don't avoid this healing time. It is Love's time with you.

Now let us be forthright as the Voice of Love. In cases of physical abuse, if you are stuck, and perhaps there are children involved as well, and you have no money to make a move, then open your heart to outside help. Go to a shelter or call a community resource center or support group for help. Plan to escape from abuse and develop a plan of action for the life you deserve. Don't allow hurt or shame to keep you stuck. Turn it around now.

It is not easy to leave abuse. Statistics show that women who enter shelters return to the abusive relationship as many as seven times before they actually step out of the relationship into love freedom.

If you are in need of this help, our healing love is with you. There are also many, many other loving people and organizations whose hearts are ready and waiting to love and help you right now.

The whole universe of love
is supporting you
as you take every single step
out of abuse

You Are In Love's Embrace

Thank you dear friend for letting us spend this time with you.

You have come to the end of our book, but, more accurately, you have come to the beginning of Love's plan for infinite expansion in your life.

You have entered the embrace of Love and there is no turning back. You can never retreat from this higher place of Light. Love won't let you. Love has you in Her tender, empowering embrace.

And so do we. We love you!

The Presence of divine Love
is unfolding right now
in your life
because
you are Love's treasure
& now
you know it!

About
The Authors

Dr. Scott Peck & Shannon Peck, among the happiest couples in the universe, are co-founders of TheLoveCenter, a non-profit educational organization "holding the space for all humanity to live in healing Love." They are authors of "The Love You Deserve: A Spiritual Guide to Genuine Love," "Liberating Your Magnificence: 25 Keys to Loving & Healing Yourself," & the audio set "All the Love You Could Ever Want!" Shannon is also author of "Love Heals: How to Heal Everything with Love." Scott is a Love teacher with a Masters in Education & Doctorate in Divinity. Shannon has her degree in Religious Studies and has been a spiritual healer for over two decades. She is also a teacher of healing.

For More Information

Visit
TheLoveCenter.com

Call
TheLoveCenter at 1-800-266-1525

E-mail
TheLoveCenter@aol.com